Advance Praise for *Blessed Youth*

"Sarah Griffith Lund draws on the wisdom of experience, expert insight and a profound faith in the immense value of our youth to spur us to action on destigmatizing mental illness. She gives us tools to carve a path forward to mental health for babies, children, teens, parents, families and the institutions and professionals who care for them. If you are searching for the words to talk to and about youth and mental health, Sarah leads by example. *Blessed Youth* is a book for parents, grandparents, teachers, pastors, mental health clinicians, everyone and anyone who cares about making the future brighter for a generation facing so much. It is past time we value children's mental health as much as we do their physical, academic and social achievements. What a gift it would be if their inheritance was the world Sarah paints for us." —**Ellen O'Donnell, PhD, Child Psychologist and Author of** *Bless This Mess: A Modern Guide to Faith and Parenting in a Chaotic World*

"Sarah Griffith Lund has blessed us three times with her wisdom and grace as she shares her own and her family's journey with mental illness. First was *Blessed are the Crazy*, then *Blessed Union,* and now, *Blessed Youth*, born out of love and pain. In *Blessed Youth* she opens her heart, and our hearts, to children and youth who live with mental illness, offering hope and a way forward to care for our children and the children in our communities." —**Hollie M. Holt-Woehl, author,** *They Don't Come with Instructions: Cries, Wisdom, and Hope for Parenting Children with Developmental Challenges*

"Sarah has gently captured the heart of how trauma and adversity impact the individual, family and community. Thus, her book helps us to break away from the toxic stigma of mental illness and reminds us that as school, organization, or church, we have the responsibility and honor to sit beside one another and be deeply present as our stories are shared and validated, and to remember that the wonderous connection to self, others, our world, and faith moves us from protection to growth." —**Lori Desautels, Assistant Professor, Butler University College of Education**

T0043514

"Through personal stories and solid research, Sarah Griffith Lund draws our attention to mental illness in young people and families and suggests concrete things that all of us—family members, friends, parents, pastors, and teachers—can do to help support those in our lives who deal with mental illness. With crisp writing and lots of first-hand accounts, this book gives insight into what it means to have mental illness or to care for someone who does. This is a helpful resource and introduction to a topic that needs more attention." —**Robert J. Keeley, Professor of Education, Calvin University, author of *Helping Our Children Grow in Faith.***

"In Sarah Griffith Lund's new book, *Blessed Youth*, she does what she set out to do: she breaks the silence about mental illness in young people. And she does so in what she calls a love letter to her niece Sydney, who died by suicide in 2020. Lund's book is accessible and gentle even though dealing with a topic that adults who love teenagers may not know much about and might even fear. Right from the very beginning of the book, she offers insights, stories, and suggestions for action while answering the question, 'are the children OK?' Although the answer to that question is a resounding, 'No!' Lund offers so much hope. This hope is founded on the promise that although the children are struggling mightily, they also know what they need. And we adults have the capacity to do much better by them. This book can help us figure out where to start." —**Dr. Emily Peck-McClain, Professor of Christian Faith Formation and Youth at Wesley Theological Seminary and author of *Arm in Arm with Adolescent Girls: Educating into the New Creation***

"In this important and grounded book, Lund opens up new spaces for understanding mental health and ill-health within the lives of children and teenagers. She pushes us to understand the complexities of mental health, and through a series of fascinating and moving stories, Sarah offers vital theological and practical strategies that can enable us to embody the love and Grace of God in our ministry with young people. Sarah Lund knows what she is talking about." —**Dr. John Swinton, Professor of Practical Theology and Pastoral Care at Aberdeen University, United Kingdom**

"Sarah Lund exhorts and equips us to listen closely to the stories of young people struggling with mental health challenges. She writes with the wisdom of a pastor, the love of a parent, and the knowledge that comes from firsthand experience. This timely resource is important for ministers, parents, teachers, and anyone who cares about the mental well-being of young people." —**Michael Paul Cartledge II, Institute for Youth Ministry, Princeton Theological Seminary**

"We are living in an unprecedented time where youth have so many social, academic and internal pressures that demand attention and excellence from them. There's no wonder that we are facing a mental health crisis amongst our young people. Rev. Sarah Lund opens the door for caregivers of various backgrounds and youth to have honest dialogue and seek professional help where needed. By weaving together her personal and professional experiences with mental health, Lund invites all of us to see ways we can be a partner on the journey for those we love and care for. *Blessed Youth* is easy to read, understand and engage with." —**Rev. Trayce L. Potter, UCC Minister for Youth & Young Adult Engagement**

"In her book, *Blessed Youth: Breaking the Silence About Mental Illness with Children and Teens,* Sarah Griffith Lund not only provides resources and actionable tools for youth, families, educators and faith communities, but she also provides poignant stories from individuals who have their own lived experience as loved ones who are caregivers and professionals. This work, dedicated to her late niece Sydney, who died by suicide, is also personal in nature for Rev. Dr. Lund. Her passion is evident as she shares her own reflections of losing a loved one who was and always be a Beloved child of God." —**Karl Shallowhorn, Director of Youth Programs, Mental Health Advocates of Western New York**

"Sarah's clarion call to offer understanding and compassion to individuals struggling with mental illness and her reminder that we do not have to be alone in this struggle is the voice we all need to hear when it comes to mental health. Her ability to weave personal story alongside practical ideas and guidance is truly Spirit-led. The invitation to provide safe (blessed) spaces in our churches, families, and schools along with her insistence that we empower youth themselves for this work is a message that can, and will, change lives." —**Rev. Patricia S. Watson, Associate Pastor, First Saints Community Church, Mental Health First Aid Instructor**

"What do you do now that mental illness has broken into your home like a thief in the night and robbed your child of joy?" "How can we live in a world where there are twelve youth suicides every day?" These are the hard questions that Rev. Dr. Sarah Lund addresses with wisdom and compassion in *Blessed Youth.* Breaking the shame and silence around mental illness, she identifies best practices to guide pastors, parents and grieving communities of faith. Speaking from the heart, without judgement, Lund models the ministry of presence for all who suffer, and all who mourn." —**Dr. Felicity Kelcourse, Associate Professor, Christian Theological Seminary and author,** *Human Development and Faith: Life-cycle Stages of Body, Mind and Soul*

"Our kids are not okay. Our children and youth are hurting!" Those who know this are also hurting. This honest book shakes us out of any lethargy we might have about the plight of our youth's mental health. It is a crisis. The personal stories told and solid research bear witness to that reality. As a tribute to Sarah's sixteen-year-old niece, Sydney, who died by suicide, this book underscores that 'to tell the true story is to heal.' This is both a touching way to start our conversation as well as to enrich those who have already been moved by experiences of mental illness. What do you need to know? How do you need to act in order to help? Sarah offers specific steps to take and resources to use to address the silence about mental illness, and above all things, to support the mental health of our youth. The book tangibly engages us in our families, in our schools, and in our faith communities to embrace our youth with our listening, our understanding, and with our actions. Weaving stories with information and compassionate action will touch everyone who reads this compelling book." —**Rev. Alan Johnson, co-founder of the Interfaith Network on Mental Illness**

"Thank you to Sarah for this timely, practical, personal book about youth and mental health. From a faith perspective, it is exactly the kind of reading that faith leaders, parents/guardians, educators, and even youth themselves can read and put into use in every day life. As a minister and parent myself, it is encouraging and refreshing to hear her voice speaking out on the importance of Mental Health." —**Rev. Catherine Stuart, Regional Minister for Children, Youth, and Young Adults, The United Church of Canada**

" 'And how are the children?' Sarah Lund has written another book, *Blessed Youth*, that draws upon her own experience to give us wise counsel. She reflects on the loss of a beloved niece, Sydney Elise Griffth, capturing her niece's zest for life and the promise of a life that ended far too early. Sarah looks through her personal lens to describe the plight of youth who face mental health challenges and our role in helping them. This is a poignant tribute to her niece; a way to let her niece live past her time with us. It is also a look at the desperate place so many young people find themselves while trying to address their own mental health. Lund concludes by offering ways we can all move to action. 'And how are the children?' We all have a part to play in answering that question with a sense of urgency. Begin now by reading *Blessed Youth*." —**Doug Beach, President, National Alliance of Mental Illness, San Antonio**

BREAKING THE SILENCE ABOUT
MENTAL ILLNESS WITH
CHILDREN AND TEENS

BLESSED YOUTH

SARAH GRIFFITH LUND

**chalice
press**

Saint Louis, Missouri

An imprint of Christian Board of Publication

ChalicePress.com

Print: 9780827203204

EPUB: 9780827203211

EPDF: 9780827203228

Printed in the United States of America

Contents

Preface

Kasserian Ingera?: And How Are the Children?

Among the most accomplished and fabled tribes in Africa, no tribe was considered to have warriors more fearsome or more intelligent than the mighty Masai. It is perhaps surprising then to learn the traditional greeting that passed between Masai warriors. "Kasserian ingera," one would always say to another. It means, "And how are the children?"

It is still the traditional greeting among the Masai, acknowledging the high value that the Masai always place on their children's well-being. Even warriors with no children of their own would always give the traditional answer, "All the children are well." Meaning, of course, that peace and safety prevail, that the priorities of protecting the young, the powerless are in place, that Masai society has not forgotten its reason for being, its proper functions and responsibilities. "All the children are well" means that life is good. It means that the daily struggles of existence even among a poor people, do not preclude proper caring for its young.

I wonder how it might affect our consciousness of our own children's welfare if in our culture we took to greeting each other with this same daily question: "And how are the children?" I wonder if we heard that question and passed it along to each other a dozen times a day, if it would begin to make a difference in the reality of how children are thought of or cared for in this country…I wonder if we could truly say without any hesitation, "The children are well, yes, all the children are well."

— Excerpted from a speech given in 1991
   by The Rev. Dr. Patrick T. O'Neill,
   First Parish Unitarian Universalist Church, Framingham, MA.

How Are the Children? A Reply

Taken from the U.S. Department of Health and Human Services
Press Release issued December 7, 2021[1]

U.S. Surgeon General Issues Advisory on Youth Mental Health Crisis Further Exposed by COVID-19 Pandemic

Today, U.S. Surgeon General Dr. Vivek Murthy issued a new Surgeon General's Advisory[2] to highlight the urgent need to address the nation's youth mental health crisis. As the nation continues the work to protect the health and safety of America's youth during this pandemic with the pediatric vaccine push amid concerns of the emerging omicron variant, the U.S. Surgeon General's Advisory on Protecting Youth Mental Health outlines the pandemic's unprecedented impacts on the mental health of America's youth and families, as well as the mental health challenges that existed long before the pandemic.

The Surgeon General's advisory calls for a swift and coordinated response to this crisis as the nation continues to battle the COVID-19 pandemic. It provides recommendations that individuals, families, community organizations, technology companies, governments, and others can take to improve the mental health of children, adolescents and young adults.

"Mental health challenges in children, adolescents, and young adults are real and widespread. Even before the pandemic, an alarming number of young people struggled with feelings of helplessness, depression, and thoughts of suicide — and rates have increased over the past decade." said **Surgeon General Vivek Murthy**. "The COVID-19 pandemic further altered their experiences at home, school, and in the community, and the effect on their mental health has been devastating. The future wellbeing of our country depends on how we support and invest in the next generation. Especially in this moment, as we work to protect the health of Americans in the face of a new variant, we also need to focus on how we can emerge stronger on the other side. This advisory shows us how we can all work together to step up for our children during this dual crisis."

Before the COVID-19 pandemic, mental health challenges were the leading cause of disability and poor life outcomes in young people, with up to 1 in 5 children ages 3 to 17 in the U.S. having a mental, emotional, developmental,

---

[1]"U.S. Surgeon General Issues Advisory on Youth Mental Health Crisis Further Exposed by COVID-19 Pandemic," U.S. Department of Health and Human Services [Press Release], December 7, 2021, https://www.hhs.gov/about/news/2021/12/07/us-surgeon-general-issues-advisory-on-youth-mental-health-crisis-further-exposed-by-covid-19-pandemic.html

[2]"Protecting Youth Mental Health: The U.S. Surgeon General's Advisory," U.S. Department of Health and Human Services, December 7, 2021. https://www.hhs.gov/sites/default/files/surgeon-general-youth-mental-health-advisory.pdf

or behavioral disorder. Additionally, from 2009 to 2019, the share of high school students who reported persistent feelings of sadness or hopelessness increased by 40%, to more than 1 in 3 students. Suicidal behaviors among high school students also increased during the decade preceding COVID, with 19% seriously considering attempting suicide, a 36% increase from 2009 to 2019, and about 16% having made a suicide plan in the prior year, a 44% increase from 2009 to 2019. Between 2007 and 2018, suicide rates among youth ages 10-24 in the U.S. increased by 57%, and early estimates show more than 6,600 suicide deaths among this age group in 2020.

The pandemic added to the pre-existing challenges that America's youth faced. It disrupted the lives of children and adolescents, such as in-person schooling, in-person social opportunities with peers and mentors, access to health care and social services, food, housing, and the health of their caregivers. The pandemic's negative impacts most heavily affected those who were vulnerable to begin with, such as youth with disabilities, racial and ethnic minorities, LGBTQ+ youth, low-income youth, youth in rural areas, youth in immigrant households, youth involved with the child welfare or juvenile justice systems, and homeless youth. This Fall, a coalition of the nation's leading experts in pediatric health declared a national emergency in child and adolescent mental health.

The Surgeon General's Advisory on Protecting Youth Mental Health outlines a series of recommendations to improve youth mental health across eleven sectors, including young people and their families, educators and schools, and media and technology companies. Topline recommendations include:

- Recognize that mental health is an essential part of overall health.

- Empower youth and their families to recognize, manage, and learn from difficult emotions.

- Ensure that every child has access to high-quality, affordable, and culturally competent mental health care.

- Support the mental health of children and youth in educational, community, and childcare settings. And expand and support the early childhood and education workforce.

- Address the economic and social barriers that contribute to poor mental health for young people, families, and caregivers.

- Increase timely data collection and research to identify and respond to youth mental health needs more rapidly. This includes more research on the relationship between technology and youth mental health, and technology companies should be more transparent with data and algorithmic processes to enable this research.

Surgeon General's Advisories are public statements that call the American people's attention to a public health issue and provide recommendations for how it should be addressed. Advisories are reserved for significant public health challenges that need the American people's immediate attention.

~~~~~~~~~~

Hello, reader, this is Sarah, the author.

I've framed Dr. Murthy's advisory report as a reply to the traditional greeting "how are the children?" But this reply, while well-grounded in research, is not the only one available to us—the parents, family members, teachers, youth leaders, and faith community members who value our nation's children.

We can also choose to reply, "Many of our children are unwell…but they are blessed youth because they are loved unconditionally by God." We have the power to change the narrative of today's mental health crisis. Our children and teens, too, hold more power than we give them credit for sometimes. For one thing, they can tell us how they are feeling and what they need. With God's help and everyone working together, we can listen to them.

We can choose to dedicate our time and energy to making mental health conditions better for our youth. We can come together and enact the Surgeon General's recommendations. More than that, we can embody actions that will bless youth. This book is a guide for how to bless our youth.

As you read this book and contemplate what your role may be in the blessing of our children's mental health, I encourage you to take your time with the stories. Yes, we face a mental health crisis and the need to respond is urgent, but we must bring our whole and best selves as we respond. One way we can stay whole, as care providers and as advocates, is to take care of ourselves. Parts of this book may bring up intense emotions for you. That is ok. As you feel the need, put aside the book until you are ready to pick it up again. I strongly encourage you to read this book in community with others so you can talk about it and share your thoughts and feelings. Pay attention to your body as you read and how you feel. This self-care is part of the collective healing work, too.

We can do this, together.

1

Blessed Youth

I am writing *Blessed Youth* to break the silence about mental illness.

I want to answer the fundamental human question "How are the children?" through the lens of mental illness. How *is* the mental health of our children?

Mental health challenges, regardless of whether they are due to a diagnosed condition or not, affect the brain and the entire body. Medical professionals have identified over three hundred types of mental illnesses, and most can be treated through a combination of talk therapies, medications, and behavioral changes. Mental illnesses are complex physical health conditions; they can be caused by a combination of factors including environment, genetics, epigenetics (when behaviors and environment cause changes to the way our genes work), events, medical conditions, and various unknowns. Since many forms of mental health challenges have a genetic causation, they can present themselves as early as infancy, childhood, or adolescence.

Mental illness touches all of us, in the form of our own personal mental health challenges, illnesses of a loved one, a coworker, or a friend. Here are some key statistics about mental illness compiled by the National Alliance on Mental Illness.[3]

1 in 5 U.S. adults experience mental illness each year

1 in 20 U.S. adults experience *serious* mental illness each year

1 in 6 U.S. youth aged 6–17 experience a mental illness each year

50% of all lifetime mental illness begins by age 14, and 75% by age 24

Blessed Youth is part of a global and intergenerational movement to break the silence about mental illness. Today's youth are generally more comfortable talking openly about mental health than older generations. Still, the stigma and shame historically associated with mental illness have kept too many people silent about their emotional and mental health challenges.

Stigma is a form of discrimination and can be directed towards oneself or others, and typically arises from ignorance or the fear of being bad, broken,

---

[3]"Mental Health by Numbers," National Alliance on Mental Illness, updated March 2021, https://www.nami.org/mhstats.

or unwanted. Mental illness can be a highly stigmatized health condition when misunderstood. Mental illness is not a sign of weakness or failure, however. Mental illness is a common part of human life.

Shame is the feeling of humiliation and is often felt as a deep sense of embarrassment. Shame comes from thinking that we are to be blamed for being or doing something wrong. It is a shadow that keeps us silent and afraid to talk about what we are experiencing. Shame can lead us to withdraw from others and prevent us from seeking help. There is no shame in having mental illness.

Blessed is a word that honors our whole story. Blessed means we are more than the shame and stigma. Blessed means we are more than the labels. Blessed means we are holy and whole. We are blessed.

The good news is that today's youth generally experience less stigma and shame around mental illness than previous generations thanks to the work of mental health advocates and educators. The problem is not with youth. The issue lies with many adults experiencing shame and stigma, being overwhelmed by a sense of failure and fear and not knowing how to help the youth who are experiencing mental health challenges. The problem is often within the systems (health, family, schools, faith communities) that are failing to successfully meet the mental health needs of youth.

We, as adults and parents, often don't know how to help youth because it is difficult to know what is going on inside their minds and bodies. Christine is a colleague of mine who works as a licensed youth mental health counselor. She says that in her practice many of the youth report feeling as if they cannot talk to their parents about their mental health challenges. If youth are not able to talk openly and honestly with parents, telling us what they are thinking and feeling, then parents feel an added pressure to know the warning signs of mental health challenges. The signs can look a lot like typical growing pains, moodiness, or hormonal changes. How do we tell the difference between developmentally appropriate behaviors, such as emotional meltdowns, and signs of mental illness, such as a panic attack?

Another reason we don't know how to help is that, even when youth do tell adults about their mental health challenges, we often don't listen closely enough or for long enough. Sometimes we are distracted or overwhelmed or tired or too busy to listen. When we do tune in, we sometimes don't believe what we are hearing, or we deny what the child or teen is saying. These responses can arise from our discomfort. What if helping requires skills and knowledge we don't have? Our responses can also arise from fear, or resentment (we might think, no one cared about *my* mental health back then), or simply from not knowing how common it really is for people to experience mental health challenges.

Christine says that the most helpful way to listen to youth is to try not to overreact or over insert yourself into the child's story. As soon as we hear about something challenging, like being bullied at school, it's natural to be reminded of something we went through growing up and we might even be triggered. Yet the key is to stay focused in the present and actively listen to the child. She says that she hears youth being discouraged when parents immediately shift the conversation to themselves, saying something like, "Well, when I was growing up, I experienced [fill in the blank]." Child clinical psychologist Dr. Becky Kennedy says, "Feelings don't scare kids. Being alone with feelings scares kids. Talking about feelings doesn't make them worse. Talking about feelings makes them manageable."[4]

Our role as adults is to listen and, according to child clinical psychologist Dr. John Duffy, to "bear witness to our child's story."[5] We bear witness to the stories of children and youth when we give them our full, undivided attention. To be a witness means being fully present and open to hearing the truth, even if it is painful. The power of bearing witness to a child's story is in creating space for our children to express their feelings and emotions as they make meaning of their experiences.

Not only do we adults have a hard time listening, but we also struggle to pay close enough attention to the warning signs, or we miss the warning signs altogether because we don't know what those signs look like in children and teens. Sometimes, even when the warning signs are there, we don't want to admit it because of our shame and fear or because of the stigma of mental illness. It can be difficult for us parents to accept the realities of mental health challenges in our children.

This book explains how to listen to youth when they do talk openly about their mental health, how to watch for signs that there is a problem, and what to do to get support. It is a resource for the whole community: families, adults in helping and support roles, and for anyone who cares about the mental health of our youth. The more people who make mental health a priority for our young people, the better for all.

This book is a guide for how to get the conversation started. I invite you to take what is useful and share it, and to leave behind what is not. Add your own ideas, thoughts, and most of all, stories and dreams. Your story matters. My story is only one story, but it is not the *only* story. I speak from my lived experiences as a person with privilege—a white, heterosexual cisgender woman who is a highly educated, middle-class, mainline Christian, wife

---

[4]Dr. Becky Kennedy, "Good Inside," *Facebook*, October 15, 2021.
[5]Dr. John Duffy, "Your Teen for Parents," (webinar from Inside Scoop with Sue, October 21, 2021).

and a mother. The world is a better place with your story and your life in it. I hope this book will encourage you to break the silence about mental illness in your life, in your family, and in your communities. The world needs to hear your stories. We especially need to hear the stories of people with personal lived experiences of mental illness.

Getting started in breaking the silence about mental illness is what's difficult for many of us. But in fact, it's ok for adults to be uncomfortable and stumble through conversations with our youth about mental illness. Youth show grace towards us if we are willing to take the risk of sounding foolish. Surely it's worth that risk to help save lives.

I am writing *Blessed Youth* as a person with lived experience of mental illness. I grew up with serious mental illness in my family and, it turns out, in myself as well (although no one knew about it). Thinking back to my childhood in the early 1980s, I know that some of my behaviors are what today would be labeled as symptoms of complex post-traumatic stress disorder. As a young child I repeatedly pulled out my hair in big clumps, I used my fingernails to harm myself and others. I wet the bed until age 11, and I had constant abdominal pain. I remember my mom taking me to see the doctor about my stomach pain and the conclusion being "nothing's wrong." For some reason the adults in my life didn't link this physical symptom and pain to my emotional pain and mental health challenges.

As a child, to hear "nothing's wrong" was not comforting. It was not good news to me because I knew that something *was* in fact wrong. I was ashamed that I wet the bed. I remember waking up to the rancid smell and feeling the cold, wet bedsheets sticking to my body. I remember the tortuous pain of my burning scalp as my own fisted hands ripped away clumps of hair. I remember the stinging feeling as both of my palmed hands burned with the red crescent marks of my fingernails digging into my skin. I remember screaming. I remember my body hurting just below my heart, feeling twisted, gutted out, and aching deep inside. I remember feeling deeply ashamed.

I remember these things as happening *to* me instead of my choosing to do them to myself. There's a difference! As a child, I felt no control over these self-harming behaviors; instead, they appeared as escape routes that I fell into, like an emergency slide used to exit a burning building.

Yet the adults in my life said there was nothing wrong with me.

Since this is what the adults told me, I went along with that story. Instead of trusting myself, I trusted them. Instead of giving voice to my own truths, I believed what they said about me. Instead of listening to my own body, I listened to them. This was how I learned to keep silent about the things that hurt me most.

By not acknowledging or validating my pain, adults taught me that pain was shameful and needed to be covered up, hidden, and kept secret. There was no one in my childhood who said, "Tell me the story of where it hurts." I kept silent about mental illness because that's what my family, my school, and my church showed me was the right way to be a good girl. Nothing ugly, painful, scary, or embarrassing was supposed to be talked about. Those things, after all, didn't really exist. And if they did, they were simply "all in your head."

Now, four decades later, I realize that what was in my head was real and was manifesting itself in physical pain and self-harm. I was processing all the trauma I experienced living in a household where there was serious and chronic untreated mental illness. My father lived with bipolar disorder and refused any treatment. My oldest brother Scott lived with bipolar disorder, too, and wasn't diagnosed and given treatment until his senior year of high school. My environment growing up at home felt unsafe and emotionally distant. My mother loved me and I know she loved me, but there is no amount of a mother's love that can protect a child from the trauma of family members with untreated serious mental illness. It's not that my mother and father didn't love me, it's that I didn't feel emotionally safe enough to receive that love.

As adults, we don't realize how profoundly our own struggles and challenges affect our children and their development. If I could go back in time, I would have done anything to get my dad the mental health support he needed. So much pain and agony could have been avoided if only he had gotten help. Tragically, his mental illness included the symptom anosognosia, which is when your own brain blocks self-awareness and self-insight. My dad didn't believe he had a mental illness because his own brain was protecting itself from this realization. Sadly, it didn't protect me as a child.

On some level, I am writing this book to my former self, a child who wished the adults in her life had known how to better read her body language, how to draw out from her stories about where it hurt, how to get help, and how to make her feel safe.

I can't go back and change the past. I can't save my father from paranoid thinking. At various times he thought he was the victim of a communist plot or feared that Satan was out to destroy our family. I can't save my father from the grand delusions of saving the world or from his violent rages triggered by voices in his head. I can't save my father even now— because he is dead.

I've tried saving my brother from the bipolar disorder that disables him, but it turns out I can't do that either. He lives with daily thoughts of suicide, with thoughts of self-harm and feelings of worthlessness.

Our father's physical, emotional, and verbal abuse contributed to my brother's mental illness. As a teen when my brother's mental health got bad, while screaming he would rage around the house, punching walls and kicking in doors. This was just how things were at our house. I would lock myself in my room. Then the door would get kicked in. There was nowhere that I felt safe.

Luckily, my brother got mental health treatment when he was suicidal and was hospitalized for the first time at age 17. My mom had to call 911 when my brother threatened suicide in the house. It was a scary time for all of us because we never knew what was going to happen next. When would the next outburst, crisis, or episode happen? Especially as the little sister and youngest of five children, there was nothing I could do to make things better. I couldn't save my brother from our father's abuse or the destructive thoughts of his own brain.

But I *can* save myself from the haunting stories of the past that beg me to go back in time to fix what was broken. Instead of sweeping up shattered glass on the kitchen floor with bare hands, I now realize there's a better way to clean up the mess, a way that won't hurt as badly and won't make your heart bleed. This is another way, a way forward with hope.

I survived the difficulties of my childhood and am now in active recovery from complex post-traumatic stress disorder. I am in regular talk therapy, spiritual direction, marriage therapy, family therapy, and under the care of a holistic health physician.

How was I able to find this hopeful way forward? One pivotal event was the day that I learned about ACEs—Adverse Childhood Experiences—in a professional development workshop, and took the survey. According to the American Society for the Positive Care of Children, a non-profit centered on improving the lives of children, ACEs are

> Potentially traumatic events in a child's life that can have negative and lasting effects on health and well-being. These experiences occur before the age of 18 and are remembered by that child as an adult. Such traumatic events may include psychological, emotional, physical, or sexual abuse; violence against mother; or living with household members who were substance abusers, mentally ill, suicidal, criminal or imprisoned. Maltreatment (child abuse, sexual abuse, neglect, bullying, etc.) causes chronic stress that can disrupt early brain development, and the development of the nervous and immune systems.[6]

---

[6]"Get the Facts Adverse Childhood Experiences (ACEs)," American Society for the Positive Care of Children, https://americanspcc.org/get-the-facts-adverse-childhood-experiences/.

It turns out I have several of the indicators of developing mental health issues based on my adverse childhood experiences. Learning this was both discomforting and liberating. Something clicked and I felt seen. I felt believed. I felt heard. I felt that my pain mattered. My pain mattered so much that it shaped who I am today—a survivor seeking an abundant life and called to partner with others to share hope and healing. Today I am no longer defined by my pain; I am defined by my hope.

Blessed Youth is a way forward with hope. It is a way for us to be open to listening to our children and teens and to pay attention not only to what their words are telling us, but also their bodies and their behaviors. Mental health is physical health. Our brains are part of our bodies, connected to everything we think, feel, say, hear, learn, do, and know. Mental health is at the center of who we are as human beings. With something as important as mental health, isn't it strange that, as a society, we've ignored and misunderstood it for so long?

I am writing *Blessed Youth* as a pastor. Having served congregations in New York, Minnesota, Florida, and Indiana, I've got a pastor's heart that longs to share hope and healing with people. My training for ministry includes a graduate degree in social work, a professional emphasis I chose because I think the best chance we have to make the world a better place is by working with communities to bring about positive change. Mental health is a spiritual and physical reality. Spirituality is where I find hope when all seems lost. Spirituality can support our holistic health because its practices reflect how we are created in the image and likeness of God, body, mind, and spirit.

I am writing *Blessed Youth* as a mother. Not only am I the daughter and sister to persons living with mental illness, I also live with a mental illness and so does my husband. Together we've made a family that includes one child. Our child has inherited qualities from both parents, including our strengths (creativity, kindness, intelligence, and openness in loving) and our challenges (anxiety, depression, and feeling stressed). Starting at a young age, we proactively began providing professional mental health support to our child starting with play therapy. As a mom, I believe that just like having a dentist, every child needs a therapist and sometimes a psychiatrist.

We are discovering how multi-generational mental health challenges shape our family. Scientific research suggests that many of the most common mental health challenges are caused by genetics and run in families, specifically bipolar disorder, schizophrenia, depression, anxiety, autism, and addictions.[7] While many of these mental health conditions

---

[7]Emily Deans M.D., "Genetic and Mental Illness," *Evolutionary Psychiatry* (blog), *Psychology Today*, September 30, 2019, https://www.psychologytoday.com/us/blog/evolutionary-psychiatry/201909/genetics-and-mental-illness.

create serious challenges in families like mine, there are gifts, skills, and personalities that run in the family too. I am grateful for the creativity, intelligence, courage, energy, passion, vision, kindness, compassion, sensitivity, and generosity that runs in my family.

I am writing this book for my child and for my child's children. When mental illness runs in families like mine, it's important to be open and honest about our family stories of mental health. Bruce Perry and Oprah Winfrey's book, *What Happened to You? Conversations on Trauma, Resilience, and Healing*,[8] invites us to share the stories that shape who we are. In this groundbreaking book, professor of psychiatry and child trauma specialist Dr. Perry explains why the stories of what happen to us also tell a story about the biology of the human brain. Intergenerational trauma changes the brain. Our mental health is impacted by what happens to us in the womb, as newborns, and as young children when our brains are rapidly developing.

Telling the stories of what happened to us creates space for compassion, empathy, and support. This approach of personal storytelling as a method of healing affirms my experience that to tell the true story is to heal. *Blessed Youth* is for all the children who never asked to be born into families whose DNA includes mental illness. In my first book about my family's history with mental illness, *Blessed are the Crazy*,[9] I talked about how I felt "crazy was in the blood" because it was evident that, genetically speaking, we all experienced various expressions of mental illness. Not talking about mental illness was just as painful as having mental illness. It was time to begin telling the stories and breaking the silence.

I am also writing *Blessed Youth* as an aunt. If nothing else, this book is a love letter to my late niece, Sydney, who died by suicide on November 2, 2020, at the age of 16. Just as I couldn't save my dad, I couldn't save her life either, and that's perhaps the greatest tragedy of all. I showed up twenty-four hours after her death and stood in the place where she took her last breath. Surrounded by the echoes of her pain, I was totally helpless to bring her back to life.

Standing in the shadow of the valley of death, I felt shocked, heartbroken, horrified, angry, confused, exhausted, and overwhelmed. How could my beautiful, brilliant, courageous, kind, and strong young niece be dead?

Sydney was open with me about some of her mental health struggles. In one of the last in-depth conversations we had about her mental health

---

[8]Bruce Perry and Oprah Winfrey, *What Happened to You? Conversations on Trauma, Resilience, and Healing* (New York: Flatiron Books, 2021).

[9]Sarah Griffith Lund, *Blessed Are The Crazy: Breaking the Silence About Mental Illness, Family, and Church* (St. Louis, MO: Chalice Press, 2014).

she talked about her attention deficit hyperactivity disorder (ADHD). Sydney's parents did the right thing by getting her into therapy and getting her ADHD medication as a child. Before she died, she asked the school guidance counselor for help. The morning of Sydney's suicide, she texted her mom that she wanted to return to therapy.

Why did Sydney die? The answer is unknowable. I want to know how to prevent another youth from dying by suicide. I want to ask, "How can we save your life?" I want to ask, "What did we do wrong?" "How could this have happened?" "Will you forgive us?"

I want to blame Sydney's death on someone. I wonder whose fault it is that she died. Out of shock, I wonder how this was possible. Who did this? Why?

For youth who die by suicide, I wonder, "What if?" What if people had listened more closely? How could we have inclined our ear to hear the whispers of a suffering mind?

How could we have seen the mental and emotional pain that was sometimes invisible? How could we have noticed what was sometimes hidden? How could we have better witnessed what was painful to see?

How could we have helped? So many unanswered questions! Most of all, I wonder, was it partially my fault? The painful answer is yes. I am part of the problem.

I am so sorry, Sydney, for not seeing the whole you. Instead, I saw the teen I wanted to see. I am so sorry, Sydney. I love you. Thank you for helping me write this book. *Blessed Youth* is dedicated to you.

It's high time to see, listen to, and support youth mental health. It's high time to break the silence about mental illness with children and teens. It's past time for too many. We have no time to lose.

We can be mental health advocates. My dream is to save our youth, youth like Sydney. I know that's ambitious, but we're in an emergency. Our children are dying. According to the Centers for Disease Control and Prevention, suicide is the second leading cause of death for people ages 10 to 34.[10]

We can use the findings of the 2021 *Addressing the Youth Mental Health Crisis* report[11] to energize us toward reversing the crisis facing our youth. This report, published by the nonprofit advocacy group Mental Health America, uses numbers to tell a story that needs to be common

---

[10]"Facts About Suicide," Centers for Disease Control, last reviewed August 30, 2021, https://www.cdc.gov/suicide/facts/index.html.

[11]"Addressing the Youth Mental Health Crisis: The Urgent Need for More Education, Services, and Supports," Mental Health America, https://mhanational.org/addressing-youth-mental-health-crisis-urgent-need-more-education-services-and-supports.

knowledge and part of our dinner table, classroom, newsroom, and social media conversations. The report provides factual grounding for policy initiatives—for example, increasing focus on mental health literacy and social and emotional learning in schools—that advocates, families, mental health professionals, and educators can bring to their state legislatures and other bodies, such as school boards. You'll find the results highlighted here and referenced throughout the book so that you too can be informed. (From here on out, I'll refer to it as "the Mental Health America report," although the organization does publish many other reports in addition to the one on the youth mental health crisis.)

To recover from the mental health crisis, we need more than numbers and statistics. We also need stories and faces. We need to feel the depth of this crisis in our bones. We need to feel first before we can heal.

How are the children, you ask? Our children are not well. Our children are not ok. Too many of our children are dying from mental illness. Now it's up to all of us to work together to help save the children.

What I want to know now is: Why are *you* reading *Blessed Youth*? And more importantly, *for whom* are you reading it? I want this book to change your life. I want this book to save a life. To do this, we need to take everything we are learning and apply it to the children that we love.

How are the children entrusted to your care? Take a moment now to think of their names and imagine their faces, the sounds of their voices. What makes you laugh when you think of them or remember them? What makes you cry? Who is coming into your mind?

Write their names down. This book is for you and it's for them, too.

This book shares personal stories from my life along with stories of families and friends. In the stories I share, some of the identifying details, such as a person's name, have been slightly altered to protect their privacy. Breaking the silence about mental illness with children and teens is the work of every family, starting with mine. That's why I go first. I share here so that you know you are not alone. Through my stories, I encourage you to connect to your own stories. I hope you will find ways to share your stories with others whom you trust.

This book shares science-based research about mental illness to help us understand how what has happened to us in our lives and our experiences changes our brains and impacts our health. The stories about mental illness reflect an important trend in our society that science helps us track. What story does the data tell us about children and teens and mental illness? When we ask the question "How are the children?" let's see what the numbers can tell us.

What the Best Mental Health Research
Says About our Blessed Youth

Mental Health America was founded in 1909 and is the nation's leading community-based non-profit resource for education, advocacy, and support for mental health. In the summer of 2021, I began serving on its board of directors and read this new report published in July 2021, *Addressing the Youth Mental Health Crisis: The Urgent Need for More Education, Services, and Supports.*[12]

According to the report, youth mental health and well-being increasingly constitutes a public health crisis. The COVID-19 pandemic accelerated and compounded that crisis. Despite this urgent need for quality, affordable, and accessible mental health care for youth, public policy has been slow to respond to this emergency, on both state and national levels.

Here are a few key insights from the report:

- Youth ages 12 to 17 are experiencing 100 percent higher rates of major depression than ten years ago

- Children's visits to the emergency room for mental health conditions increased significantly from March 2020 to October 2020

- Black and Latinx children are less likely than white children to receive treatment for depression, even though they experience the same, if not higher, rates of depression

- Black and Latinx youth reported the largest increases in suicidal thinking from 2019 to 2020

- Native American youth and those self-identifying as multiracial youth ages 11 to 17 reported the highest rates of depression

The good news is that some states and schools have enacted policies requiring mental health education, services, and supports. New York was the first state to require K-12 mental health education, followed by Virginia and then Florida.

Minnesota and Kansas have programs encouraging school-based mental health services provided by community partners. Telehealth services are starting to be used as an important tool to expand access to mental health care in school settings.

---

[12]Sydney Daniello et al., "Report: Addressing the Youth Mental Health Crisis: The Urgent Need for More Education, Services, and Supports," Mental Health America, https://mhanational.org/addressing-youth-mental-health-crisis-urgent-need-more-education-services-and-supports.

Oregon passed the first bill in 2019 to allow excused absences for mental and behavioral health issues. Other states have followed including Colorado, Maine, Utah, Connecticut, and Virginia.

The personal stories and testimonies of youth themselves have led the way to this change. Students trained in advocacy reached out to their legislators and used their own voices and power to create new laws to support mental health education and services in schools.

What We Can Do for Our Blessed Youth

What can we adults do? As parents, faith communities, as school and wider community members, how can we help our blessed youth?

First, we can educate ourselves. We can learn the early warning signs and learn the best early intervention techniques. This will take intentional effort, education, and training specific to mental health challenges of children and youth. Mental Health First Aid is one of the nation's best educational training programs and can help educate you about children and youth mental health.[13] In Mental Health First Aid training you learn that, in addition to signs of being a danger to self or others, what makes mental illness different from what might be considered acceptable mood changes or behaviors is the persistence and length or duration of the mood. Two weeks or more of sustained moods that are disruptive to one's abilities to function at home or at school or with friends are reasons to be concerned.

When it comes to detecting early signs of mental illness, the best option is to err on the side of caution and talk to a doctor if the behaviors or moods are concerning or persistent. This is the same approach we take when a child has concerning or persistent signs of a physical illness such as a cough or fever. Ideally, we wouldn't let them cough or have a fever for two weeks without taking them to see a doctor.

Consider signing up for a Mental Health First Aid course, either by yourself or with a group, just as you would when you need to certify or refresh your first aid, CPR, or water safety/lifeguarding certificate.

Second, we can take care of our own mental health. As we become more mentally healthy, our children will benefit. In my own family, we all are actively seeking mental health support knowing that mental illness is a family system dynamic since we are all interconnected. When I am doing better mentally as parent, my child will be better for it. Going to therapy and taking medications as prescribed is good parenting. Child psychologist Dr. Daniel Siegel in his book *The Whole-Brain Child*[14] says, "As parents

---

[13]Mental Health First Aid, https://www.mentalhealthfirstaid.org.

[14]Daniel Siegel, *The Whole-Brain Child: 12 Revolutionary Strategies to Nurture Your Child's Developing Mind* (New York: Bantam, 2012).

become more aware and emotionally healthy, their children reap the rewards and move toward health as well. That means that integrating and cultivating your own brain is one of the most loving and generous gifts you can give your child."

Third, we can advocate. It's ok if you haven't had any formal advocacy training yet. A great way to continue your learning journey and become an advocate is to identify communities of like-minded others, either locally or online with groups like National Alliance on Mental Illness (NAMI), to learn what efforts are already underway to help our youth.

Find out what mental health resources are available in your child's school, or in the district where most of your community's youth attend school.

- What does the school district, or your county or state already provide in terms of mental health education, access to services, and mental health excused absences?

- How extensive is mental health screening in schools, and what kinds of peer support are available?

- What programs are shown to improve early intervention in youth mental health?

Upstream from these specific issues are some larger, more encompassing ones. Think of all the resources we allocate for our youth, through our systems of education: health care; after-school care; food support; music, theater, sports, and recreation opportunities; and so on. Assuming equal access to these resources (a big assumption), are children from some communities graduating high school at higher or lower rates? Do some experience higher or lower levels of chronic disease or mental health challenges?

What social structures exist in your community that shapes how youth assume leadership roles? If you live in a community with many professionals and leaders or if such people are among your circle of friends or your coffee gathering at church, then your blessed youth have built-in access to leadership examples and opportunities. If your community or circle of friends is several steps removed from people in power or leadership examples are lacking, then it's likely that your blessed youth need extra resources to be able to step up and have their voices heard.

Maybe now is the time for you to learn about health and school outcomes for youth from various backgrounds, including LGBTQ+ (Lesbian, Gay, Bisexual, Transgender, Queer, Plus) and BIPOC[15] (Black, Indigenous, and People of Color) youth. What efforts are already underway to improve

---

[15]LGBTQ+ stands for lesbian, gay, bisexual, transgender, queer, and others who may identify in various ways in the gender and sexuality dimensions of their lives. BIPOC stands for Black, indigenous, and people of color. Both terms are evolving.

equity in outcomes? What might be your role in supporting equity? Are there ways you can promote youth leadership or provide resources to your local school for such leadership programs?

At the end of this chapter, I've provided some additional research highlights about child and teen mental health. This data can help you get started on your research if you're ready to jump (or dip your toe) into advocacy and action steps now.

What You Will Learn in This Book

If you need to spend a little more time on storytelling and study before delving into advocacy, I encourage you to do so. In fact, spending time in personal reflection and in sharing stories with your blessed community is more than just a good idea; it's an essential part of your advocacy journey. That is why I have chosen to present this book in a particular format: a mix of facts, personal stories, reflection, learning opportunities, and suggestions for action steps.

In the next chapters you will learn how parents, schools, faith communities, and others can partner to share hope and healing for children from infancy to age 18 who are experiencing mental health challenges. Each chapter focuses on both the challenges and the opportunities we all have in the midst of the mental health crisis facing youth today. Together we can listen, be advocates, and help build a world in which our children are loved and heard.

We can use the institutions—schools and churches, and possibly others—to bless the mental health of our youth. Through them, we can:

- Create educational opportunities for youth and their families
- Connect youth and their families to accessible, affordable, and quality community mental health care
- Provide empowerment training for youth in self-advocacy (to find their voices and tell their stories)
- Create spaces for youth peer support—a proven method to save lives

As adults, we can challenge and hold one another accountable to listen to our youth and affirm them. We can bring change to community institutions such as schools and faith communities. We can prioritize mental health by changing our behaviors and attitudes towards youth to help create environments and systems in which the mental health of youth and families will feel safe and flourish.

Blessed are the youth who live with mental illness. They are the constellation of stars in our collective night sky. Born into existence, coming out of chaos, they shine a great light in the shadows. Will we take the time to slow down, pay attention and truly see them? We dedicate this work to them.

Important Research Highlights About Children and Teen Mental Health from the 2021 Mental Health America Report

- By a substantial margin, mental health conditions and self-harm are the greatest contributors to the burden of disease for young people. In 2019, for people ages 5 to 19 in the US, mental health conditions and self-harm contributed 23.1 percent. Asthma (6.5 percent) and road injuries (6 percent) are the second and third contributors

- Rates of depression, anxiety, and thoughts of suicide are all increasing

- Deaths by suicide among youth increased by over 30 percent between 2014 and 2017

- The average age at which youth are dying by suicide is getting younger, especially among Black youth

- When surveyed, youth ages 14 to 24 said they need the following mental health supports: (1) better access to mental health professionals—direct care—in school, (2) mental health breaks as part of work or school, and (3) learning about mental health

- In 2019, 16 percent of youth ages 12 to 17 reported experiencing a major depressive episode in the past year compared to 8 percent in 2009, double the previous rate

- Rates of children's emergency department visits related to deliberate self-harm increased 329 percent between 2007 and 2016

- COVID-19 worsened these alarming trends in children and teens. From March to October 2020, children's visits to the emergency room for mental health conditions increased 31 percent for those 12 to 17 years old and 24 percent for children ages 5 to 11 compared to the same period in 2019

- Youth are searching online for help for mental health. Mental Health America's online screening tool saw a 628 percent increase in use in 2020 with nearly 1 million youth ages 11 to 17 taking the online screening. Throughout the COVID-19 pandemic, youth ages 11 to 17 have been more likely than any other age group to score for moderate-to-severe symptoms of anxiety and depression. Of those who took the screening for anxiety in 2020, 84 percent of 11 to 17 year-olds scored with symptoms of moderate-to-severe anxiety, and 91 percent of the youth who took the screening for depression scored 7 percent and 9 percent higher than the rates among adults over 18 for anxiety and depression respectively

Increasing mental health disparities: LGBTQ+ and BIPOC

- Rates of suicidal ideation are the highest among youth, especially LGBTQ+

- In 2019, 46.8 percent of youth that identify as LGBTQ+ reported seriously considering suicide, more than three times the rate of youth identifying as heterosexual (14.5 percent)

- In 2020, over half (51 percent) of 11 to 17 year-olds reported having thoughts of suicide or self-harm more than half or nearly every day of the previous two weeks. Rates of frequent suicidal ideation were even higher among LGBTQ+ youth, with 62 percent reporting frequent thoughts of suicide or self-harm

- In 2019, 25.5 percent of American Indian or Alaskan Native youth, 11.8 percent of Black youth, and 8.9 percent of Hispanic youth reported engaging in suicidal behavior in the past year in 2019, compared to only 7.9 percent of white youth

- There has been a rapid increase in suicidal behavior and suicide deaths among Black youth, especially Black boys and younger Black youth over the past decade

Trends in Access to Care

- 43.3 percent of all youth with a major depressive episode received any mental health care treatment in 2019

- 67 percent of youth of color who need mental health help still do not receive care

- 50.3 percent of white youth, 35.6 percent of Black, and 36.8 percent of Hispanic youth who needed care received mental health services in 2019

- Youth of color are more likely than white youth to receive mental health services in educational setting as opposed to specialty medical settings. School-based care reduces barriers such as transportation and health insurance that disproportionately impact youth of color. Increasing access to school-based mental health services can promote equity and reduce disparities in access to mental health care

Action Items to Help our Blessed Youth

- *Promote mental health literacy curricula that inform youth about mental health conditions, wellness skills, and how to seek help.* Studies show that mental health education generates positive and meaningful outcomes that reduce suicide attempts, suicidal ideation, and substance abuse.

- *Advocate for professional mental health services in schools.* In 2019, the ACLU released a report detailing the lack of school mental health personnel using data by the Department of Education and noted that 14 million students were in schools with a police officer but no counselor, nurse, school psychologist, or social worker. Over 90 percent of schools failed to meet professional standards for school counselors.

- *Empower youth to help plan and lead the mental health education experience for their peers.* Youth are aware of their own mental health challenges and those of their peers and are interested in mental health education. A 2019 Pew Research survey found that anxiety and depression are at the top of the list of challenges teens see among their peers. In a survey of teens ages 13 to 17, 70 percent said that anxiety and depression were major problems among themselves and their peers, outranking other significant problems such as bullying, substance use, teen pregnancy, and poverty. Because teens are aware of the challenges and recognize them, they may be quite motivated to learn about mental health in order to increase their own ability to recognize signs and symptoms and to get help.

- *Support youth-led initiatives.* Youth empowerment is a key strategy with youth-led initiatives that are responsive to the immediate needs of young people and that reflect what they have articulated and believe is going to help. Youth know what interventions they need right now to improve their mental health and well-being.

- *Provide safe space for empowerment and encouragement.* The key to youth empowerment is to give them the space and encouragement to ask for what they need. Ask young people not just what the problems are, but also how they want to see them solved and how they can play a key role in accomplishing that.

- *Equip peer-to-peer support programs.* Data indicate that youth are more likely to talk to a friend than to anyone else when experiencing mental health symptoms. Some schools (and churches) are beginning to offer peer support programs, which allow for early conversations and access to support from students from diverse backgrounds. Peer connections are critical resources for children and teens.

2

Blessed Children

Did you know that a baby can be born with a mental illness? While speaking at a mental health education event at First Congregational Church in Columbus, Ohio, I heard another presenter from Nationwide Children's Hospital share the results of research showing that newborns can exhibit early signs of mental health challenges. According to the Mayo Clinic, "Many mental health concerns have roots traceable to challenges occurring in infancy and early childhood, and early interventions for these developing minds are necessary to prevent future mental health disorders."[16] The good news about the mental health movement is that we are in an era today of new focus on infant mental health and child psychiatry.

It's common for many first-time parents to frantically try to comfort and calm their day-old babies, while no one is getting sleep, and everyone is upset. Newborns with mental health challenges are often irritable, restless, and in real emotional pain. Mental health concerns in infants can look like the following:[17]

- Poor sleep patterns
- Difficulties with feeding
- Persistent or unremitting crying
- Restlessness
- Gastric disturbance
- Anxiety and tension
- Distress and fear
- Lack of weight gain or failure to thrive
- Failure to meet expected developmental milestones

As a new mom myself in 2009, I noticed that my baby showed some of these behaviors. When I asked the pediatrician about them at his check-ups, I learned they were considered somewhat common and not cause

---

[16]"Infants Have Mental Health Needs, Too," Mayo Clinic Health System, April 20, 2021, https://www.mayoclinichealthsystem.org/hometown-health/speaking-of-health/infants-have-mental-health-needs-too.

[17]Ibid.

for real alarm because they probably just marked a "phase" in my child's development. The doctor was sympathetic and compassionate, but busy and didn't have much time to spend with me. The message I heard was that if my baby was displaying certain behaviors, it was not a big deal. Maybe the problems were all in my head. Maybe the problems were my fault as the mom.

I know I wasn't alone. When I was able to get out of the house and connect to other new moms, I found that we all seemed to be struggling with lack of sleep, stress, anxiety, and sadness. There is so much shame and guilt for mothers who aren't happy and who can't seem to make their babies happy. At my baby shower, I received a popular book that suggests ways to ensure my baby is "the happiest baby on the block." The key strategy to making babies happy was swaddling, which works for some babies, but not mine. Once again, I felt like I was doing something wrong. Turns out, lots of babies do not respond well to swaddling. Still, for many parents, books and videos by "baby experts" like the one I received end up being our first introduction to the feeling that there is something wrong with us and our babies.

Sandy, a member of my congregation, struggled to comfort her first baby, who always seemed to be fussy. She wondered if her baby might be anxious or depressed. While Sandy admits that some of the baby's unhappiness probably came from her own transference of stress as a new mom, she also noticed that the baby became much happier when they switched from breastmilk to a soy-based formula. The baby was fussy because of digestive and intestinal pain related to allergies and being lactose intolerant, and not because Sandy doing anything wrong.

Celiac disease is not uncommon in newborns and is another reason why some babies are unhappy. It can cause weakness, low body weight, and severe abdominal pain. Babies with celiac disease can scream nonstop at birth and throughout their first months of life until they are diagnosed and action is taken so that their pain can be addressed. Luckily, Sandy got help and resolved the issue, but for many parents, it is too embarrassing to admit there is a problem, let alone ask anyone for help. The trauma this experience causes to both the baby and to the parents is significant. Early days of bonding are disrupted, and it is difficult to develop close attachments.

Parenting books and media depictions of life with a newborn often paint a rosy picture of how things will be once our bundle of joy arrives in the world. Regardless of whether the problem has its roots in mental health challenges or something else, it is always hard to hear we are doing something wrong—or just to see that we don't fit the rosy picture—when we are obviously trying our best. Even though we have good intentions as parents, when we are under stress, sleep deprived, and overwhelmed, our behaviors can cause trauma to our newborn's developing mental health.

I remember sitting in the pediatrician's office holding my newborn, in tears because he wasn't gaining weight. My mother tells the story of her holding me as a newborn and my father looking at her and asking, "Is that baby getting smaller?" It turns out that as an infant I had trouble gaining weight too. In fact, I was losing weight.

I am the youngest of five children. Our mother gave birth to all of us in a period of six years. So, her body was understandably depleted and exhausted. My mother's efforts to breastfeed me were sabotaged by stress. She tried her best, but sometimes even our best is not enough. My mom literally had nothing more to give.

For infants, bonding with caregivers promotes positive mental health. In early childhood circles this is also referred to as social and emotional development. According to the professional organization Zero to Three:[18]

> Social and emotional development, or infant and early childhood mental health (IECMH), is the developing capacity of a child from birth to 5 years old in the context of family, community and culture to:
> - Form close and secure adult and peer relationships
> - Experience, manage, and express a full range of emotions
> - Explore the environment and learn

When babies are irritable and fussy, it can make it challenging for caregivers to bond with them, causing harm to both the baby's and the caregivers' mental health. This example demonstrates how the whole family system's well-being and mental health are intricately connected.

My friend Shawnna lives with mental illness and recently gave birth to her second child. She was hospitalized for a mental health crisis in the first week after delivery. With the help of hospitalization, medications, and intensive therapy, Shawnna says she's starting to feel better "after getting lost in my brain for a bit." She says, "It's nice to feel more like myself every day."

Shawnna is helping to break the silence about mental illness as a mother of two children. After being discharged from the inpatient psychiatric hospital, she wrote in a public social media post about her experience with mental health challenges, pregnancy, birth, and parenting. She gave me

---

[18]"How to Talk About Infant and Early Childhood Mental Health," Zero to Three, March 12, 2019, https://www.zerotothree.org/resources/2674-how-to-talk-about-infant-and-early-childhood-mental-health.

permission to share this with you here. Her reason? She says, "I want people to know how real and hard it can be. It is so much worse this time around and there are days when I feel like I'm drowning." She says she is grateful for her husband, saying, "I would not be here if it weren't for him. He and my doctor finally convinced me to do therapy and I'm so hopeful it will pull me out of this hole." Shawnna posted the following on social media:

> Someone told me a few years ago that postpartum depression and postpartum anxiety would likely be worse if I had another child—and they were right. Add post-traumatic stress disorder (I was officially diagnosed about a month ago) and you have the perfect storm of madness going on inside my brain. I'm now afraid of the dark and it's still really hard to be by myself. Any sudden loud noise or movement makes me jump.... I hope all of that goes away soon. Medication and intensive therapy have saved my life. Thank God for psychiatrists and medication.

Breaking the Silence about Children with Mental Illness in our Families

It is not a moral failure to have an unhappy baby, but it can make you unpopular. It is shaming and stigmatizing to be excluded just because your baby often fusses and seems crabby. Best-selling baby books insist that if we try hard enough, we can make our babies happy. But what if our baby has a mental illness or another condition that is affecting their social and emotional development? What if we simply don't understand what they want to communicate to us through their behavior? No amount of wishing, praying, singing, rocking, kissing, swaddling, or nursing will cure our baby under such circumstances.

Breaking the silence about mental illness and our struggles to cope begins early in life. It begins when we acknowledge the following:

- Mental illness in babies is not all the parent's fault.
- Mental illness in children is not all the parent's fault.
- Medical conditions in babies and children are not all the parent's fault. These and other problems that lead to difficulty in forming bonds are not the mother's fault.
- Adult disabilities and mental illness are not all the fault of the parents, either. Do parents with disabilities or mental illness love their children? Yes.
- We want to blame someone when something goes wrong, yet most parents do not intentionally cause their children trauma. We do not wrap up mental illness in a package with a red bow and put it under

the tree for our child. We don't want to give our children mental illness. Yet sometimes we do pass along mental illness to our children because, like it or not, it is part of our DNA.

The second step in breaking the silence is to acknowledge that the first weeks with a baby might not be a particularly happy experience, and that this is ok. As our babies grow, they may begin to show signs of mental health challenges or a medical condition that needs attention. Or there may be nothing technically "wrong" with them, but the parent is still stressed out or concerned over whether that poop is the right color! This is normal. Yet many times parents do not have the information or resources to get the support their families need.

The early days at home with a baby are often isolating, with very little contact with others. Lack of support from others only makes the struggles with mental health worse. It's a sign of wisdom to reach out for help and for answers. If the pediatrician doesn't seem to be taking our questions seriously, maybe we need to use our network and find referrals to a new doctor's practice, or to lean on other supportive parents.

As friends and family, it is helpful to consider what the parent(s) want instead of what we want. We need to put the new parents' needs first. Maybe we envision our visit to the newborn's home going a certain way; instead, we'd do better to drop any specific expectations and ask the new parent what they want and/or need. Do they want a nap, knowing the baby is in good hands? Does our friend want help with housework and errands so they can have some time alone with baby, free of those worries? Does our sister want someone to take the baby to the park so she can have an hour of feeling "normal" again, just puttering around, doing chores, or taking a shower? We need to be ready to help the way that the new parent defines help.

The third step in breaking the silence is to have compassion. Mental illness in babies and young children can be caused by substance use of the parents. Yet, with deeper understanding of how addictions change the brain, science is now showing us that substance abuse is itself a mental illness.[19] No one chooses to have a mental illness. No one gives their baby mental illness on purpose since it can be part of our genetic predisposition.

If a baby has a mental health challenge because of a parent's drug use, this is still not the mother or the father's fault alone. Again, there is no one person to blame. The parents didn't make their baby sick on purpose. What made the baby sick is our broken society that causes people to suffer from poverty, racism, sexism, homophobia, and so on, so that people are in dire

---

[19]"Substance Use and Co-Occurring Mental Disorders," National Institute on Mental Illness, last revised March 2021, https://www.nimh.nih.gov/health/topics/substance-use-and-mental-health/.

distress and pain. Drug use is often a response to pain and an attempt to numb the hurt. Substance use can lead to addiction and become part of a harmful cycle. People who use drugs need our compassion and support.

I have seen firsthand how maternal substance abuse hurts babies and young children. One mother in my extended family used drugs throughout her pregnancy and now her children have significant developmental and learning disabilities, as well as mental health challenges. The babies and children did not choose this life for themselves. My extended family has worked hard to provide the extra support these babies and children need in ways that will encourage, teach, and help them thrive.

What is particularly heartbreaking is how mental illness is passed from one generation to the next. Recall that sometimes the signs and symptoms of such illness are already apparent at birth.

I wonder what it feels like to be a baby born with mental illness. I wonder if that was me? Is it possible for a baby to be born with post-traumatic stress disorder from the womb? My mom tells the story of her unplanned pregnancy with me. I am an "IUD baby." I am an "oopsie baby." My life is evidence that sometimes birth control doesn't work. To make matters worse, I was a month past my due date. My mother's water broke at home late at night.

My father drove her to the hospital and made her sit in the car until after midnight, so they would not be billed for an extra day. We had the money; he just liked to control her. I can't imagine the stress of being in the hospital parking lot, in labor, and not being allowed to enter the hospital for medical care and support in giving birth. Also, my father insisted that I would be born with brain damage because he was certain the IUD was lodged in my brain. Luckily it wasn't, but my mom had nightmares about this image throughout her pregnancy.

How did this trauma (and others) affect my mother's pregnancy with me? How did my mother's trauma form me in her womb? How did she feel being pregnant again for the fifth time with four young children all under the age of 6 at home? How did her mental health impact my mental health? Was I born with a mental illness?

Research into intergenerational trauma shows that at some point three generations share the same bloodstream at the same moment in time.[20] Your grandmother, pregnant with your mother, carried you inside of her body when you existed in your mother as an egg. Read that sentence again. Read that sentence out loud. Boom.

---

[20]Rachel Yehuda and Amy Lehrner, "Intergenerational Transmission of Trauma Effects: Putative Role of Epigenetic Mechanisms," *World Psychiatry* 17, no. 3 (September 7, 2018): 243–257, https://doi.org/10.1002/wps.20568.

We carry inside of us the traumas of our mothers and grandmothers. Our DNA is imprinted with the stories they were too ashamed to tell. Breaking the silence about mental illness liberates us from carrying the pain of our ancestors in our blood and interrupts the cycle of intergenerational trauma.

In a post for the United Church of Christ's *Vital Signs and Statistics* blog on the topic of Black infant mortality and poor outcomes of pregnancy for Black women, Rev. Lee Yates, a pastor who focuses on social justice, says:

> Researchers and advocates are looking at the life experiences of these mothers and the generational experience of Back women. The amount of stress from explicit and implicit racism takes a toll, and that is dangerous to both the pregnant mother and child. Racist structures that give different treatment regardless of a person's resources or education are also a factor that limits care. Toxic stress from the trauma and humiliation of racism and prejudice that Black women face daily is the cause.[21]

Articles and scholarly work on generational trauma are becoming more common, adding another layer to the conversation. Science Magazine published an online feature on this topic in 2018 and many others have followed. We now know that trauma can carry forward into future generations, and the historic and present trauma of Black mothers is undeniable. We cannot undo past trauma, but we can be aware of its consequences and do our best to respond with compassion and healing.

As mentioned in Chapter 1, helping our blessed children can also happen through advocacy. We can vote and speak out on policies that support babies, toddlers, and their families. Zero to Three and similar organizations provide resources to help you learn about local, state, and national-level policies affecting child mental health.[22]

Breaking the Silence about Children with Mental Illness at Church

It's important to break the silence about mental illness not only in our homes, but also in our houses of worship. Many faith communities dedicate special time for the education of children. Sometimes this happens during worship, sometimes it happens as part of children's Sunday school. What if we talked about mental illness with our children as part of faith formation? What if we talked to our young children about how

---

[21]Lee Yates, "Infant Mortality, Trauma Education, and the Importance of Transformation," *Vital Signs & Statistics* (blog), *The Center for Analytics, Research & Development, and Data for the United Church of Christ*, June 22, 2020, https://carducc.wordpress.com/2020/06/22/infant-mortality-trauma-education-and-the-importance-of-transformation/.

[22]"Policy & Advocacy," Zero to Three, https://www.zerotothree.org/policy-and-advocacy.

there is no emotion or feeling that is shameful or bad? What if we helped to end the stigma and shame around crying in public, no matter how big or old we get and no matter our gender? What if we told our children that even God cries?

We can break the silence about mental illness with children at church by telling stories about God's care for our mental health. Here is an example of how to give a message. It's based on one I wrote in 2020 for Mental Health Sunday, which many congregations recognize during May (Mental Health Awareness Month).

When God Cries

Desmond Tutu's beloved children's book *God's Dream*[23] describes a young boy who cries when he realizes that his selfish actions have caused a rift in a friendship with a classmate.

Tutu writes that God cries, too, when we hurt others and are ourselves hurt. I'm taken by this sentiment of God crying with us; and by the message that God is not too holy to feel. God is not above emotion, but God is below—with us.

We find God alongside us in the depths of our suffering; God cries, too. In my children's sermon about mental health, I show the children a small, unopened package of tissues. I ask a volunteer to open the package and share with us what they discover inside. Carefully a tissue emerges from its package.

Then I ask for a tissue from the child. I share that I need it to wipe my eyes because I have been a little teary that morning. We talk about how when we have big feelings that don't have words, they come out as tears. I share Tutu's book, showing them the page where the boy is crying.

I read to them about how when we are crying, God cries, too. We talk about how tissues are also used when we are sick and have a runny nose, a bad cold, or a sinus infection. Sometimes when we are very sick, we go to the doctor and get medicine.

Our brains, just like our hearts and our lungs, need to be healthy. But sometimes when we are not feeling good, we also go to see a doctor. I share that my brother went to the doctor because his brain was not feeling good. The doctor gave him medicine to help him feel better.

Now my brother is home from the hospital and his brain is doing better. Mental health means taking care of our whole body,

---

[23]Archbishop Desmond Tutu, *God's Dream* (Somerville, MA: Candlewick Press, 2010).

including our brain. When our brain is healthy, we feel better. Sometimes we cry when we are feeling sad. And when we cry, God is with us.

When we are sick and not feeling good, God is with us. We are never alone because God is always with us and loves us no matter what. God loves us even when we cry and when we feel sick, not only when we are happy and feel healthy.

We can offer God this prayer together:

Thank you, God, for tears that express how we are feeling. Thank you, God, for our brains that help us know your love. Thank you, God, for mental health and for people who help us feel better when we are sick. We love you: help us to love each other. Amen.

Breaking the silence about mental illness in community is powerful. It teaches our children that this is a community to which they can bring their whole life, their whole being, and their whole unfolding story. It tells our children that we love them no matter who they are, how they are feeling, or where they are on their life's journey. Whether it is our sacred stories from our traditions or our family stories, children learn through storytelling. Telling stories that normalize healthy approaches to mental health empowers the whole community and is transformative.

Beginning the Transformation: Tell Stories

Storytelling can lead us to a deeper understanding of family dynamics involving mental health. Telling our family's stories about mental illness is important because it uncovers the truth about who we are and it leads to deeper healing. Children with symptoms of mental illness are linked to the stories of their family's mental illness. I wonder what stories the symptoms of mental illness in children tell us about ourselves and our families.

For example, children in my extended family have been diagnosed with attention deficit hyperactivity disorder (ADHD). The primary symptoms include difficulty focusing and trouble with impulse control.[24] These children are smart and energetic and are not intentionally acting naughty. Their presence fills a room with sound and movement. Often, children with ADHD get punished for "bad behavior" and "not following the rules"—meaning rules about sitting still and keeping quiet.

Why do we expect young children to have the power to control an overwhelming impulse in their brain that is telling them to move and talk? It's like telling a starving person not to eat or drink anything. It goes

[24]"Attention-Deficit/Hyperactivity Disorder (ADHD) in Children," Mayo Clinic, June 25, 2019, https://www.mayoclinic.org/diseases-conditions/adhd/symptoms-causes/syc-20350889.

against their most deeply embedded desires. For kids with ADHD, "bad" behavior and breaking the rules is not their fault. They don't want to be "bad." The children are expressing part of who they are and how they are feeling in their bodies and minds.

When adults in authority view children living with mental health challenges as bad children who break the rules, it hurts children and breaks their hearts. Being judged as "bad" is profoundly shameful to them and their families. Judgment, discrimination, and punishment for the symptoms of mental illness is traumatic for children and makes them even more sick. Mental illness is not a choice. Our children do not choose to get sick.

Too often we punish children for having mental illness instead of addressing the mental health issue that is causing their behaviors. Black boys with disabilities are at heightened risk of getting disciplined in schools compared to their white able-bodied peers because of combination of racial bias and discrimination against children with disabilities.[25]

Increasing numbers of young children are getting sick with mental illness. Especially since COVID-19, more children than ever before are showing symptoms of mental illness, continuing an alarming national trend. According to the previously mentioned special report from Mental Health America, from March to October 2020, children's visits to the emergency room for mental health conditions increased 24 percent for children ages 5 to 11 compared to the same period in 2019.[26]

It hurts to acknowledge the untold stories of suffering these numbers tell. Our youth are not ok. Our children are hurting physically and mentally. The pain is real. What kind of intergenerational trauma from COVID-19 will our children be passing on to the next generation?

Our hospital and healthcare systems are not equipped or prepared to provide quality, affordable, and accessible mental health care to young children entering the emergency room with a mental health crisis. In 2021, when a child in my extended family went to the emergency room to get help after expressing thoughts of suicide they had to wait in the ER overnight just to get a bed in the pediatric psychiatric unit. Even then, we found that this locked children's psych unit was simply a short hallway located right off the adult unit. Hospitals that are generally not designed

---

[25]Valerie Strauss, "Implicit Racial Bias Causes Black Boys to Be Disciplined at School More Than Whites, Federal Report Finds," *Washington Post*, April 5, 2018, https://www.washingtonpost.com/news/answer-sheet/wp/2018/04/05/implicit-racial-bias-causes-black-boys-to-be-disciplined-at-school-more-than-whites-federal-report-finds/.

[26] "Addressing the Youth Mental Health Crisis: The Urgent Need for More Education, Services, and Supports," Mental Health America, https://mhanational.org/addressing-youth-mental-health-crisis-urgent-need-more-education-services-and-supports.

to care for children's mental health needs are being forced to create space for more beds wherever they can. In one local hospital where I live, beds are being placed in storage closets.

The young children waiting in the ER for psychiatric care have names and faces that sound and look like your family members and neighbors. The tragic reality is that the children who made it to the ER are the lucky ones who got the help they needed to stay alive. Many young children are thinking about suicide and are engaging in self-harm without getting any help at all.

When I asked my young family member about what they wanted parents to know about mental health and youth, they said that depression is the biggest issue. They said that depression is "everywhere." Depression in children is a growing problem that kids are starting to recognize in themselves and their peers. The leading risk factor for suicide in children is the presence of depression.

The alarming new evidence shows that starting as young as five years old, a time when many children are entering kindergarten, mental illness begins to be one of the greatest risks to their health and well-being. According to the report by Mental Health America introduced in Chapter 1, "Mental health conditions and self-harm are the greatest contributors to the burden of disease for young people by a substantial margin. For people ages 5–19 in the USA in 2019, mental health conditions and self-harm contributed 23.1%, asthma (6.5%) and road injuries (6%) the second and third."[27]

My family's story supports this cold, hard truth that even at a young age children can start vocalizing their thoughts of suicide. Such remarks can begin with a child simply acknowledging that they don't want to live anymore. A member of my church who is now in her eighties and survived a lifelong battle with mental illness shared that on her seventh birthday she told her parents she wanted to die.

What do you do when your young child tells you they don't want to live? What do you say? How do you recover from that gut punch? How do you help your child recover? What happens when their words fall into the shadowy pit of your own despair and get lost in the depths of your own pain? How do you ride out the silence that follows such a devastating acknowledgment of the truth of childhood mental illness? What do you do now that mental illness has broken into your home like a thief in the night and robbed your child of joy?

One of the hardest moments as a parent came one autumn night, when we told our eleven-year-old child that his sixteen-year-old cousin Sydney

---

[27]Ibid, 11.

had died earlier that day by suicide. We collapsed into one another's arms. Losing a loved one to suicide, especially someone so young, is one of the most disorienting experiences I've ever had. It's challenging as a parent to navigate how to tell children when a family member dies by suicide.

In the moment, I briefly wondered whether to explain to my child the method of how Sydney died. But I know from mental health training that it is better not to give any details about the way she died. By explaining the details of the death, you paint a mental picture of how someone can die by suicide. This may plant a seed and provide a person the knowledge of how to plan their own suicide. Safe messaging after a suicide means that we don't give any details. Instead, we simply share that the person "died by suicide." I know the details, but it wasn't safe or responsible to tell my child. This is not about keeping secrets; it is about keeping children and vulnerable people safe.

I also learned not to say "committed suicide" because this language is too closely associated with committing a crime. Suicide is the result of a mental illness and mental illness is not a crime. The best language to use is to say someone "died by suicide" just like you would say that someone died from cancer or a heart attack. We would never say someone "committed cancer," right?

I learned it is important to name suicide as the cause of death because this helps break the silence about mental illness. My friend and United Church of Christ minister Rev. Dr. Rachael Keefe wrote the book *The Lifesaving Church*[28] about how faith communities can help both prevent suicide and support families experiencing suicide loss. When Sydney died, I reached out to Rachael and asked her to hold our family in prayer. She prayed with me over the phone and reminded me of the importance of acknowledging the complexity of suicide loss. There are no simple answers.

After talking with Rachael, I realized that I needed to ask Pastor Mark, the minster of our family's home church, to say the word "suicide" at least once during my niece's memorial service so that as a family we could begin to acknowledge the collective sorrow of being survivors of a suicide loss. When Pastor Mark said the word "suicide" out loud during the eulogy, I felt a shift in the room, a recognition of the true story, a way to name the cause of our unbearable pain. Pastor Mark's sensitive care, compassionate listening, and his faithful presence in the midst of our sorrow helped us in a time of unspeakable loss.

There is deep shame in families related to suicide, especially the suicide of a child. Shame comes from feeling that we failed as parents and as

---

[28]Rev. Dr. Rachael Keefe, *The Lifesaving Church: Faith Communities and Suicide Prevention* (St. Louis, MO: Chalice Press, 2018).

family members. This shame can be toxic for our own mental health and well-being, adding another layer to the complex grief during a time of tremendous loss. There is also shame associated with blaming ourselves for our child's death.

When stories such as these do arise, it is important to state that suicide is not the fault of survivors. Suicide is complex. Suicide loss survivors often feel guilty, but it is not their fault. When a child dies by suicide, it is not the mother's fault. When a child dies by suicide, it is not the father's fault. When a grandchild dies by suicide, it is not the grandparent's fault. When a child in the family dies by suicide, it is not the family's fault. As much as we want to know the root cause of suicide, there is no simple answer.

When there is mental illness and especially when there is suicide, we want to know why. Telling the story of "what happened to you" can help us begin to understand why. In the first few days after Sydney's death, my child kept asking me why his cousin died. Her suicide is one of the most traumatic events in his childhood and in my life.

My son loved her, and as an only child, he looked up to her as a big sister. Why did she die? We don't know. Why didn't she get the help she needed? We don't know. We may never know the answers to these questions. And not having answers is itself another kind of death, its own journey through the valley of the shadow of death. Suicide pierces the human heart. How can we live in a world where there are twelve youth suicides every day?[29]

Our children look to us for the answers to life's big questions. What happens when we can't answer them? The day you admit to your child that you really don't know, they step through that invisible portal from the land where adults know everything, and something changes in your relationship. It feels scary to admit to my child that no one knows the answers to why Sydney died and why she didn't get help and that we will probably never know the answers.

It's important to *share* stories and it is ok to end them with "we love you no matter what," or "she died by suicide," or "it's no one person's fault," or "I don't know." Dr. Becky Kennedy says that, when talking with children and processing intense or deep feelings, you can say:[30]

- "You're a good kid having a hard time."

- "I'm not scared of your feelings. I won't leave you alone when you feel this way. I love you."

---

[29]"Facts & Resources," Suicide and Crisis Center of North Texas, https://www.sccenter.org/facts-and-resources/.

[30]Dr. Becky Kennedy, "Good Inside," *Facebook*, November 10, 2021.

- "There's nothing you could do that would make me stop loving you. Nothing, nothing, nothing."

Likewise, it's important to *listen* to our children's stories. In conversation with me about children and mental health, Rev. Lee Yates shared this insight for adults talking with children on difficult topics.

> There is something to be said for asking children what they think about the issues and how they see them. Often children can have perspective and spiritual insight that we lack as adults. I remember my daughter at age 7 wondering why people were afraid of cemeteries, because all those Spirits had already sunk down into the center of the Earth, into the 'heart of God.' Children's spirituality often transcends the fears and social structures that adults have propped up to defend ourselves from reality.

Children's spirituality can indeed be powerful. Faith traditions are filled with sacred stories that we teach our young children. Sydney learned the stories of the Christian tradition and the Easter story of Jesus rising from the dead, a victory of life over death. The resurrection story teaches us that God is with us throughout our lives and beyond. One of our favorite Sydney stories comes from my sister, who tells it like this:

> When Sydney was in kindergarten, we had a back yard funeral for her betta fish. It was Easter weekend and we had found a velvet-lined ring box to use for the fish coffin. Sydney dug a hole in the back yard and tossed the boxed fish playfully on the way to the burial. I noticed that the slippery fish flew out of the box mid-air and landed in tall grass but didn't say anything to Sydney. She knelt in the grass to place the boxed fish in the dirt, then decided to say one more goodbye to her fish. I held my breath as she opened the ring box, preparing to begin the tedious search for the fish in the grass. Sydney investigated the empty box and then looked up with amazement, joyfully proclaiming, "HE IS RISEN!"

This story gives me hope that our children *do* make meaning out of death, that they *do* find hope in the resurrection. Our children's faith can flourish even in the face of uncertainty. What we can say to our youth regarding suicide is that it is a mental illness, that sometimes mental illnesses end in death, but that even that is not the end of the story. For God's love never ends. Even in death, we are loved. No matter what.

Blessing Our Children

Mental illness for young children can be terminal. Therefore education, prevention, and getting resources to families with babies and young children is essential for the mental health and well-being of all our children. Even with the high risks associated with serious mental illness, there is reason to hope. Together we can find a way forward through education, advocacy, and connecting our children and teen to resources. But first we must acknowledge the difficult truth that our children are not ok.

The time for denial is over. Ignoring how sick our children are and keeping silent about mental illness is killing our children. The fact is, we are witnessing a crisis in this nation with more young children living with terminal mental illness than ever before.

The shame, fear, and stigma that we carry as adults harm our children. We may be avoiding scheduling a mental health evaluation for our child because *we* are afraid of the results, even though we know that prevention and early detection of mental health challenges are key to positive outcomes for our youth's mental health. Or we may not have adequate health insurance and worry about the financial burden. Or perhaps we do not have a flexible employment situation and therefore struggle to make time for doctors' appointments. These are just some of the barriers families face when seeking medical care for mental health.

It can feel overwhelming to navigate what to do when our children experience a mental health crisis. We want to be able to be the ones to help our children. But it can be helpful to remember that it's not our role as parents, teachers, or other adults in a faith setting to diagnose children. It is our role to get them to a doctor or mental health professional who can diagnose and determine next steps, including evaluating whether the child needs treatment.

There is a stigma around diagnosis and medications for mental illness, especially in children. But, as adults, we cannot let our own biases, fears, and shame make the decision. It's better to be informed and empowered when it comes to our children's mental health. We can free ourselves from letting our own shame and stigma prevent us from getting our children the help they need. If you think your child may be experiencing symptoms of mental illness, schedule an evaluation for them. Early detection is key and is the best possibility for treatment and prevention of serious mental illness.

The good news is because we now know more about the mental health crisis our children are facing, we can do more. We can talk with our children about mental health, teaching them the signs and symptoms. We can connect our children with mental health resources and supports. We can provide our children with a hopeful tomorrow, working together to save lives and prevent suicide.

Young children are like hummingbirds. They are the smallest forms of humankind, yet they flutter with larger-than-life energy. Yes, they are tireless and resilient. But they also need to be nurtured with goodness and love. Their lives are being threatened by changes in their environments outside of their control. Yet no matter what challenges they face, each one is unique and a valued member of the family of creation.

Blessed are the children, for they carry inside of them the realm of heaven.

3

Blessed Teens

I've blocked out most of my memories of the 1990s—my teen years. With all the mental health challenges in my family and my own personal struggles, what I do remember is how good I felt when I was out of the house. I sought approval and encouragement in the classroom and on the athletic court and field. I threw myself into academics and sports. I became an honors student and an all-around athlete competing in track and field, volleyball, basketball, and my favorite, soccer. My sports coaches became surrogate fathers and my teammates became my family.

On weekends I trained by running for miles alone around the neighborhood. On Sundays I walked to church with my family. I read books outside in the sun. I mowed the lawn. I went to sleepovers with friends from my sports teams.

Then there was a turning point when at tryouts for the high school girls soccer team, I broke my right dominant kicking foot. During a scrimmage, another girl whacked my foot instead of the ball. At the time, both my physical and mental health were in peak condition. But that's when depression hit me the hardest.

Suddenly, my social group, my identity, and my favorite activity all came to a screeching halt. Even though I made the team, I couldn't play. I remember wearing knockoff Doc Martens boots made of fake black leather, the only kind of shoe into which my swollen foot could fit. I remember sinking into a lonely hole. I gained a lot of weight and began to feel ashamed of my body.

I self-medicated my depression with boys. I was lucky I didn't get pregnant. I kept my grades up. I kept going to church. I kept feeling sad. I kept feeling lost.

It's easy to miss the warning signs in teens like me because we don't make a lot of noise. Part of the reason I kept quiet about my mental health was because I was numb and couldn't feel much of anything. Throughout my entire childhood and adolescence, I never once saw a therapist or mental health counselor, even though looking back it's clear I needed the help. It's true that I never directly asked any adult for help. Instead, I remained silent about my pain.

During these years, my father became increasingly sick, with his own mental health rapidly deteriorating. My parents were separated for a long time before finally divorcing, and my father lived in his truck for a while back in California while the rest of us moved to Missouri. He was homeless, jobless, disabled, and living with serious, untreated bipolar disorder. I remember my father calling me on the house phone only to rant for over an hour about political conspiracies as I grew weary of his garbled talk. He didn't ask how school was going or if we were ok. The focus was always on him, his big ideas, and how hurt he was that our mother took us away from him. Being the child of a parent with untreated serious mental illness created a sense of instability and insecurity for me that's lasted my whole life.

Having such an unstable father with severe mental illness contributed to my mental health challenges as a teen. My father's mental illness caused him to neglect caring for me (physically and emotionally), which left a hole in my heart. Thankfully, through school, church, and sports, I was able to connect in healthy ways to other male role models: my art teacher, who encouraged my creative gifts, my English teacher, who stopped me in the school hallway one day and asked if I was ok, my pastor, who called me a child of God, and my soccer coach, who believed I could help the team win.

I sometimes wonder how I would be different today if I had received the mental health care I needed when I was a child and a teenager. How might counseling or antidepressants have helped me? While I never experienced suicidal ideation, the depression that started in my teens continues into adulthood. Now in midlife, I'm finally doing regular therapy dealing with my symptoms of depression and recovering from complex post-traumatic stress disorder in talk therapy sessions.

The good news is that now, three decades since my teen years, our society has made progress around mental health. Teens today don't live with the intense silence and shame as we did in the 1990s and earlier.

Mental Health and Social Media

While the silence and shame related to mental illness is not as common today among youth, today's teens live with different social norms, specifically the challenges of social media and all its pressures. Today the incredible amount of cyberbullying and the feelings of being socially ostracized online take their toll on the mental health of teens. My colleague Christine, a therapist for teens, hears her clients talk about the intense pressure and unrealistic expectations for one another to respond immediately to any question, comment, or social media post. Not doing so is taken as a sign that they don't truly care about their friends. She says their brains can't really cope with all the social pressures magnified x1000 online, pressure of always being connected and of feeling or fearing being left out if one is not always connected online.

Dr. John Duffy says in his book *A Year of Positive Thinking for Teens*[31] that social media can feed into the feelings teens have of being on an emotional roller coaster. Social media can overwhelm teens with unrealistic expectations. He says, "it's normal to have thoughts and feelings like 'this is too hard' or 'I'll never measure up.'"[32] Dr. Duffy confirms that children report significantly more stress today than ever before, along with poor self-esteem and more self-loathing.

Social media fuels so many of the anxiety and depression issues therapists see in youth. The harm caused by social media is being confirmed now because social media platforms are facing allegations of knowingly contributing to negative mental health in youth. Also, youth can get a lot of their information on social media; it has replaced the encyclopedias of the past. While it can provide accessible and helpful information, youth can also find dangerous and harmful information online, such as methods and details of suicide which is a big risk factor for teens' mental health. When it comes to social media and youth, we need to ask the question, "How are the children?" How do the children in your life engage in social media and technology? How does this contribute to their feelings of anxiety or depression?

Listening to Our Teens' Stories

Teens today have positive role models, like four-time Grand Slam tennis champion Naomi Osaka, who publicly break the silence about mental illness and advocate by example for athletes to have the right to take a mental health break. Like Osaka, Olympic star gymnast Simone Biles shocked the world at the 2021 Tokyo Games by putting her mental health first. Osaka wrote in a TIME article that she withdrew from the French Open to tend to her mental health. She says, "I don't have all the answers. I do hope that people can relate and understand it's O.K. to not be O.K. and it's O.K. to talk about it. There are people who can help, and there is usually light at the end of any tunnel."[33]

Biles withdrew from most of her Olympic competitions to focus on her mental health, meeting with a sports psychologist twice a day so that she could come back and finish strong for her last event (she won the bronze

---

[31]John Duffy, *A Year of Positive Thinking for Teens: Daily Motivations to Beat Stress, Inspire Happiness, and Achieve Your Goals* (Emeryville, CA: Rockridge Press, 2020).
[32]Ibid.
[33]Naomi Osaka, "It's O.K. to Not Be O.K.: 'Gaining Perspective,'" *TIME*, July 19/26, 2021.

medal). Around the world, people celebrated her example that self-care is more important than winning and that sometimes doing your best means taking a break.

Even with more positive role models and more mental health education and better mental health resources, teens continue to face serious mental health challenges.

Callie is a teen who lives with multiple mental health challenges. She shared with me that her journey with mental illness has not been easy, but that she's learned to "make friends" with her diagnosis. Instead of viewing having a mental illness as a negative dynamic, she views her diagnosis as just another part of her life. Callie has deep wisdom to share with us from her lived experiences. I asked her to share the top five things that adults need to know about what teens are experiencing related to mental health. Callie said the following:

(1) Teens have a strong sense of self as a part of Generation Z. Many of our generation used the COVID-19 quarantine to discover who we were, and through that exploration have been able to get in contact with psychiatrists for an official diagnosis. By taking this time, teens have come away with more empathy towards one another's mental illnesses—the constant pressure students are facing—and... great knowledge on how to help/uplift those within the mental illness community.

(2) Teens are not offended by others asking them questions; rather, they find the lack of understanding and the lack of curiosity towards what they are going through offensive.

(3) Teens are still not fully developed as adults. Many teens are open to a change in their diagnosis, but these changes can cause one to lose faith. Adults need to be aware that teens are going through triumphs and tribulations as they gain these diagnoses and work to understand what they need to be their best selves.

(4) Many teens don't see their diagnosis as a crutch, but rather as a helping friend. Throughout my diagnosis of severe anxiety and OCD, I had to explain to doctors and therapists that I did not want to rid myself of anxiety. For years my anxiety has allowed me...to understand people's emotions, predict problems with statements or ideas, and keep myself safe. My friend anxiety has allowed me to do many things in life that I couldn't see were possible without it.

(5) Adults need to be willing to enter these uncomfortable dialogues about mental health with teens/younger generations. It has

helped me and many other teens to be able to enter intelligent conversation with our elders to understand the stigma around mental health as we try to promote a positive outlook towards mental health.

I celebrate Callie's hard-earned wisdom and how her insights can help us become better advocates for teens facing mental health challenges. Through treatment, Callie was able to grow, learn, and become a whole person living with anxiety. Callie challenges adults to become educated and be prepared to have real, honest, and brave conversations with teens about mental illness. As much as we may think teens want to be independent, they still look to adults for guidance, support, and help, especially when it comes to mental health. It's our adult responsibility to be there for them.

The most important thing we can do is to listen to teens. We may assume that a teen facing a diagnosis of anxiety would be devastated and wish to be cured. Some teens may feel that way, but not all. For Callie, her anxiety is her friend and has become an important part of how she understands herself. Anxiety, according to Callie, is not all bad; there are some positive parts to it. I only know that because that's how Callie described it in her own words.

The thing about mental illness is that it affects each person differently. Anxiety is Callie's friend because she has learned how to navigate living with it, thanks to the support of treatment. Yet for someone else, anxiety might be their enemy. That's why taking time to listen deeply to each teen matters. There's not just one story about anxiety or just one story about depression in teens. Each teen is going to have their own unique stories to tell about mental illness.

Our role as adults is to help create the spaces for these stories to be told, held, honored, and respected. Our role is also to grant teens grace and space to be…teens! As Dr. Becky Kennedy says, "Our job is not to help our kids feel happy. Our job is to help our kids feel at home with themselves. Happiness naturally finds kids (and adults) who've learned it's ok to be exactly who they are."[34] Happiness is nice, Dr. Kenney says, but resilience is better. Callie urges us to remember that teens are still children. Teens may look grown-up, but their brains are still developing for several more years.

Although a teen is considered an adult at 18, their brain is still rapidly growing, changing, and morphing; it is not yet mature, even though society deems them legal adults. According to Dr. Martha Denckla, director of developmental cognitive neurology at the Kennedy Krieger Institute at Johns Hopkins University, the executive function of the brain matures

[34]Dr. Becker Kennedy, "Good Inside," *Facebook*, August 18, 2021.

at age 25 and the social brain matures at around age 32.[35] Teens are often expected to navigate the world as if they were adults when, biologically speaking, their brains are far from being fully developed.

Teens are not afraid to ask the hard questions. Callie reminds us that avoiding difficult conversations doesn't help make things better; it makes things worse. As adults, we need to get over our own feelings of inadequacy and discomfort. Teens want reassurance that there's no such thing as a stupid or inappropriate question. When engaging in conversations with teens, Dr. John Duffy advises adults to "Keep asking. Create an easy, open line of communication. Speak your piece and let her speak hers. Let the resounding thought she's left with be, 'no matter what, I've got your back.'"[36] While conversations with teens about mental illness may feel awkward and uncomfortable, we can lean into having an open mind and compassionate heart. We can trust that, for the most part, it is enough.

Teens need us to be ready to hear everything they have to say and to listen without judgment and without ascribing shame. That's why doing our own work first of educating ourselves about mental health and taking care of our own mental health needs are both vitally important if we are to help the teens in our lives. By the same token, it's ok for us adults to be honest and tell teens when we don't know the answer to something and let them know we will do our best to find the answer.

Research backs up what Callie is telling us. According to the Mental Health America report, teens are aware of their own mental health challenges and those of their peers, and they are interested in mental health education. The report highlights a 2019 Pew Research survey finding that anxiety and depression are at the top of the list of challenges teens see among their peers. In that survey, 70 percent of teens said that anxiety and depression were major problems among themselves and their peers, outranking other significant problems such as bullying, substance use, teen pregnancy, and poverty.

It's time to shift our attention away from issues that are no longer as pressing, and time to start articulating a national strategy to address the youth mental health crisis in America. Mental health providers are feeling swamped and are often drained and burnt out. The stress of the pandemic is taking its toll on mental health professionals who are scrambling to keep up with the need for services. The waitlists for getting an appointment or

[35]Kayt Sukel, "When is the Brain 'Mature'?" Dana Foundation, April 4, 2017, https://www.dana.org/article/when-is-the-brain-mature/.

[36]John Duffy, *Parenting the New Teen in the Age of Anxiety: A Complete Guide to Your Child's Stressed, Depressed, Expanded, Amazing Adolescence*, preface (Coral Gables, FL: Mango Press, 2019).

getting a hospital bed or residential treatment placement are too long. Our children don't have time to wait.

Mental health professionals are not only underpaid, but they are also overstressed from having to spread themselves so thin trying to do everything humanly possible to make care accessible to a broad range of people. But in so doing, the quality of their care often diminishes significantly.

How are teens doing, you ask? If we want to help all the people, families, children, and teens possible, then we need to make shifts in policy and social attitudes. Mental health care is vital and needs to be supported and funded. Affordable care should not happen at the expense of trained professionals being chronically underpaid and overworked. That simply leads to burnout, and the problem of not having enough care to go around is exacerbated. We need strong networks of organic, community-based resources to surround our youth.

The good news for us is that because teens are often aware of and recognize mental health challenges in themselves and their peers, they seem to be more motivated to learn about mental health so they can better recognize signs and symptoms and get help.[37] Now that mental illness is less stigmatized, people are breaking the silence about it and finding one another for peer support. This is what Callie means when she says there is a "mental illness community." Strengthening and increasing peer support just might be the key to addressing the mental health crisis in our youth. More on that later.

Teens are part of social webs that may be invisible to adults, such as social media and digital platforms. Even before COVID-19, teens were connecting online like no other generation before them. While the negative effects of social media on self-image have been well-documented, adults would do well to understand that many teens have also been able to leverage social media for good. The months of quarantine gave them few other options but to connect online for learning and for play. Teens are showing adults how community doesn't happen only in person.

Teens are leaders of the online community building movement. Many of us adults discounted the validity of online relationship networks of teens, yet because of the pandemic we needed the expertise of teens to show us how to make authentic relationships online. Teens are discovering how to encourage, support, and advocate for one another's mental health in creative and innovative ways. While the pandemic increased mental health challenges for many teens, some, like Callie, experienced it as a time to reset and renew themselves.

---

[37]"Mental Health America Report."

Yes, many things teens do online are fairly innocent. But it's our job as adults to remember that their brains are still developing. Because the brain is still developing and rapidly changing, teens are developing in ways that make teens vulnerable to seeing issues as absolute, in black-and-white terms rather than as complex, nuanced problems. We adults can encourage rest and renewal for our teens' brains.

Teens can be idealistic and can also feel hopeless about the problems of the world. However, with encouragement, support, and resources, teens can put their idealism to work for the better and can help us all begin to address the complex problems of the world. Teens who are concerned for others and who want to improve the world can harness their energy and angst in service of providing support to a world in need, or at least, to a part of that world.

According to the Mental Health America report, in the year before the COVID-19 pandemic, 16 percent of youth ages 12 to 17 reported experiencing a major depressive episode in the past year. These rates are double those of a decade earlier. Indeed, COVID-19 seems to have worsened these alarming trends in teens: from March to October 2020, teens' visits to the emergency room for mental health conditions increased 31 percent compared to the same period in 2019.[38]

My young family member you met in Chapter 2 was right when they said that depression is hitting youth hard. And it seems to be manifesting in teens even more than younger children. What does depression look like in teens? According to the Child Mind Institute, "Depression is a psychiatric disorder that afflicts young people with chronic feelings of sadness or worthlessness—the defining characteristic of the disorder is that it robs a person of the capacity for pleasure."[39] Teens who are depressed feel unfulfilled, bored, unstimulated, unmotivated, and uninspired. Depression can prevent our teens from experiencing enjoyable activities because they have lost interest. Life for a teen experiencing a major depressive episode is often joyless and lonely. Depression creates a painful emotional cycle of not feeling like being around people even while becoming more isolated and alone.

With schools closed for in-person learning in the spring of 2020 and many schools remaining close through the spring of 2021 due to COVID-19, the feelings of isolation teens normally experience were compounded significantly. It was during this period of social isolation that depression among teens became much worse. But depression isn't the only disorder

---

[38]Ibid.
[39]"Quick Facts on Major Depressive Disorder," Child Mind Institute, https://child-mind.org/guide/major-depressive-disorder/.

that affects teens so critically that a parent or other adult has to take their teen to the emergency room. The most common reasons are related to deliberate self-harm, anxiety, and substance use.[40]

As Callie reminds us, teens aren't done growing yet, and it's not just their brains that are developing, it's also the entire rest of their personhood. This includes teens' growth in self-awareness and understanding of what their gender and sexuality mean to them. Dr. John Duffy says, "Body image issues are far more prevalent now than ever before…and substance abuse is on the rise, often in pursuit of self-medication, and the nature and type of substance used are shape-shifting."[41]

As teens' bodies change, so does their understanding of their own sexuality. Many are also exploring their gender identity and sexual orientation, adding stress and confusion, making teens vulnerable to mental health challenges. Teens figuring out what it might mean for them to be lesbian, gay, bisexual, transgender, queer, or another designation may encounter additional stigma and discrimination from family, religion, school, and others. Regardless of your views on LGBTQ+ identities, it is important to note what the research tells us. How are the LGBTQ+ children?

According to the Mental Health America report, teens who identify as LGBTQ+ have the highest rates of suicidal ideation among teens. In 2020, over half (51 percent) of all teens reported having thoughts of suicide or self-harm more than half or nearly every day of the previous two weeks. Rates of frequent suicidal ideation were even higher among LGBTQ+ youth, with 62 percent reporting frequent thoughts of suicide or self-harm.[42] In addition, both transgender and non-binary youth are experiencing challenges navigating their identities without much support. According to one colleague in ministry who serves as a chaplain for a private school, transgender and non-binary students are struggling the most, especially those who are transitioning without support.

Most adults can already offer youth unconditional love and positive regard no matter what their identities; some also positively affirm gender and sexual identities that are outside the norms. A few adults, unfortunately, withhold love and support because of the way a teen articulates or expresses their identity. And tragically, there are adults who actively reject and condemn youth because of their identities. Summer Gomez at Penny Lane Center reports that unsurprisingly LGBTQ+ youth who receive neutral

[40]Gaby Galvin, "Study: Rate of Mental Health ER Visits Surges for Kids and Teens," *US News*, May 11, 2020, https://www.usnews.com/news/healthiest-communities/articles/2020-05-11/children-visit-er-for-mental-health-issues-at-increased-rate.

[41]John Duffy "Parenting the New Teen," preface.

[42]"Mental Health America Report."

or positive support do much better emotionally than youth who are condemned.[43] The suicide rates differ dramatically for these two groups. What are we to do?

Blessing Our Teens

We can support the mental well-being of our teens by creating spaces that are safe for open dialogue about human sexuality and gender identity. We can also initiate teen-friendly faith conversations around all forms of diversity or feelings of being "othered," whether due to cultural, racial, physical ability, health, or neurodevelopmental differences. I'm choosing to concentrate on sexual orientation and gender identity here because it's an area in which considerable mental health research is being done now by organizations such as The Trevor Project. How are LGBTQ+ children? As the data and the stories tell us, this is an important area in which families, schools, and faith communities may be best positioned to provide support.[44]

Teens who feel pressured to hide their sexual orientation or gender identity often experience emotional isolation, shame, and rejection. The stigma and shame of being in the closet often contributes to teens to feeling self-hatred and low self-esteem. I am passionate about how we create open and affirming communities for LGBTQ+ youth because of friends and family members I love who are LGBTQ+.

There are many people who believe being LGBTQ+ is a choice and one that can be changed. But this doesn't line up with the science. What's more, attempting to change one's gender identity or sexual orientation through conversion therapy doesn't work. Rather than help, conversion therapy methods harm vulnerable teens and families looking for ways to "change" and convert the "gay away." Even though conversion therapy methods are proven to be ineffective and harmful, many communities still allow this so-called therapy to harm our blessed youth. As of this writing, conversion therapy is still legal for adults in all fifty states, with fewer than half of all states banning the practice for youth. Does your state allow this form of psychological child abuse?

Conversion therapy was originally built on the belief that homosexuality is an illness that can be cured. Since 1998, the American Psychiatric Association (APA) has opposed any psychiatric treatment like conversion therapy, and in 1973, it declared that homosexuality is not a mental

---

[43]Summer Gomez at Penny Lane Center, www.pennylane.org.

[44] Tim Kersher, "Synod Delegates 'Deplore' Conversion Therapy, Call for Its Ban," United Church of Christ, July 19, 2021, https://www.ucc.org/synod-delegates-deplore-conversion-therapy-call-for-its-ban/.

disorder. Today, the APA encourages legislation "to prohibit the practice of conversion therapies based on the a priori assumption that persons with diverse sexual orientations and gender identities are mentally ill."[45]

The United Church of Christ (UCC) became one of the first mainline Protestant denominations to call for a ban on conversion therapy by passing a resolution that I helped to author at its 33rd General Synod in July of 2021. The UCC resolution invites us all to "advocate for state and federal laws protecting adults, youth and children" from the conversion therapy. There is a strong connection between conversion therapy and suicidal ideation, attempts, and deaths. The Trevor Project, a nonprofit whose mission is to support LGBTQ+ youth, states that 42 percent of conversion therapy subjects attempted to end their life.

My family has been directly harmed by faith communities that don't affirm LGBTQ+ youth. My heart broke as I listened to a teen in my family share how disturbing it was for them to be in a church youth group where the youth minister called being gay a sin. This experience made them feel unsafe and they began to hate church because of it. No wonder so many teens feel disconnected from the church.

The church hasn't lost these youth; it has evicted them. As a pastor, it is gut-wrenching to hear of churches treating our youth so recklessly and carelessly, severing their ties to the faith community, and even worse, damaging their sense of self-worth as beloved children of God. The trauma and harm (even if unintentional) caused by faith communities contributes to poor mental health in youth. Faith communities can also be places that provide significant support, care, and hope, as we will discuss more and explore further in Chapter 6.

What do you do when a teen tells you they are LGBTQ+? Amy Johnson, Minister for Sexuality Education and Justice on the national staff of the United Church of Christ says, "If your child comes out to you as gay, trans, non-binary, or another identity or orientation with which you aren't familiar, have the first thing that comes out of your mouth be, 'I love you no matter what. I'm here for you.'" Affirming your unconditional love for your child is the best first response.

In a conversation with me in the fall of 2021 about how to support the mental health of youth navigating understanding their sexuality, Amy said: "LGBTQ+ teens need parental support. It's one of the most crucial pieces of healthy development for them, and it's one of the largest protective

[45]*Position Statement on Conversion Therapy and LGBTQ Patients*, Psychiatry, PDF file, https://www.psychiatry.org/File%20Library/About-APA/Organization-Documents-Policies/Policies/Position-Conversion-Therapy.pdf.

factors in their life. Put any surprise or discomfort aside for the moment to assure them of your love and support. Then get any help you need to live into that more fully."

Amy echoes what we've been hearing from youth themselves about mental health: Listen without judgment. Listen with an open mind. Be open to learning what you don't already know. Get help to fill in the gaps.

The goal of mental health is not only to provide these life-saving interventions but also to offer preventative care. How can we invest in the mental well-being of teens? What does it look like to nurture the mental health of teens and make mental health a priority? This will be the focus of Chapters 5 and 6. Community institutions such as school and faith communities can work harder to support parents and families seeking to create environments for our teens to flourish. Likewise, we as individuals can help our institutions improve.

The teen years are the cocooning phase of metamorphosis, a Greek word that means "transformation." No wonder that teens can appear hidden, withdrawn, folded inward. There really is a great deal happening inside of them that we can't see. Teens need a safe place to change into who they are becoming. They need us to be patient while they grow. They need us to help them to trust themselves and to recognize their latent beauty. They need time to grow, cocooned in our love.

Blessed are the teens, for they carry inside them the power of transformation.

4

Blessed Families

In my previous books, *Blessed Are the Crazy*[46] and *Blessed Union*,[47] I break the silence about how mental illness significantly affects my own blessed family. Those books tell the stories and help to make meaning of my experiences as a daughter, sister, cousin, and wife of people with chronic and serious mental illness.

Now, as a parent and as a pastor working with families, I realize how challenging it is for parents to navigate mental health questions and concerns with our children. I knew it was time to write a book for families—this is why I am writing *Blessed Youth*.

No two families look the same. Families can be defined in terms of biology, adtoption, or other ways of formation. And I use the word "family" loosely here and respect whatever configuration works best for you. However, I insist on the term "blessed" when talking about mental illness with families because it's my way of looking for the silver lining in an otherwise gray and foreboding sky. It's my way of asking God once the storm passes through, "Where's the rainbow?" We are blessed when we tell the stories that heal us.

There's a lot of parenting advice out there, but not enough stories being told about navigating life with mental illness. There are not enough conversations about what it means when multiple members of the family live together with mental health challenges. How does a parent's depression or obsessive-compulsive disorder or anxiety or ADHD affect their parenting? What happens when both the parent and the child are experiencing suicidal ideation at the same time, as occurred in my family?

Parenting when everyone in the family lives with mental health challenge can, as author and pastor Rev. Lee Yates said to me in a conversation, be "a fight or a well-choreographed dance. It all depends on how we communicate and how much work we put into ourselves and the family."

---

[46] Sarah Griffith Lund, *Blessed Are the Crazy: Breaking the Silence About Mental Illness, Family, and Church* (St. Louis, MO: Chalice Press, 2014).

[47] Sarah Griffith Lund, *Blessed Union: Breaking the Silence About Mental Illness and Marriage.* (St. Louis, MO: Chalice Press, 2021).

The key for blessed families is to get help! It's impossible to parent well without some backup and support. Negotiating mental illness requires even more accompaniment. Dr. Bruce Perry reminds us that we aren't meant to raise children and teens alone and isolated.[48] It truly takes a village to raise our children.

Creating circles of support is especially important for single parents, divorced parents, or other adults serving as the primary caregiver, raising a child who has mental health challenges. Take, for example, my friend Wendy, a single mother who has shared custody of her children. Because the courts are involved, she doesn't always have the control or power to provide the care that she wants to give them. Wendy says, "I don't get to be a parent because everything I do is monitored by the court and motivated by legal implications. If parents are in a high conflict child custody situation, mental health providers may be intimidated and unable to use personal judgment."

Parental divorce or separation is on the list of what is considered an adverse childhood experience or ACE. It puts children at additional risk for mental health challenges. Yet often divorce and separation are unavoidable and the best option for the overall well-being of the family, even if it might lead to poorer short- or long-term mental health outcomes for children. Rather than make divorced, separated, or single parents feel guilty about this possibility, my intention is quite the opposite: to prompt you to get you and your children help and to feel good about doing so.

My parents' divorce is one of the ACEs that led to my personal mental health challenges. My healing from complex PTSD has come from spending time with my therapist breaking the silence about intergenerational mental illness. In my family, we can easily trace four generations of chronic mental illness going back to my great grandparents on my father's side.

What I've noticed is that the first generation was silent about mental illness. The second generation denied mental illness. The third generation (my generation) is the first one to talk about it openly and break the silence. The fourth generation is getting early detection, evaluation, and treatment. My dream for the fifth generation is that they'll benefit from early prevention efforts, starting in the womb.

To that end: What if we began to think about family planning as an exercise in preventative mental health? What if the standard practice for genealogy and family tree depiction included open acknowledgment not only of who died or suffered from cancer and heart disease, but also who died or suffered from chronic mental illness or suicide? Breaking the silence

---

[48]Bruce Perry, *What Happened to You?*, 75.

about mental illness can be a gift that blesses families who are at elevated risk for mental health challenges due to genetics.

What if the culture around baby showers included books and resources to support maternal, paternal, and infant mental health? What if we gave every expectant parent a poster for the nursery that depicted the full spectrum of human emotions, encouraging early development of emotional intelligence and self-expression?

What if the culture around family leave took the mental health of the whole family seriously? What if paternity and maternity leave benefits at minimum included an additional two weeks after the return to work to be used as needed for mental health days, and could be taken at any time within the first twenty-four months of the baby's life? What kinds of blessed families would we be if our society prioritized mental well-being for all parents—especially mothers of color, who experience the additional stressors of systemic racism and trauma?

When we think about family mental health, we need to consider the mental well-being of both the parents and the children. Sleep deprived, depressed, and anxious parents are going to be too stressed to provide optimal emotional support to children.

We have experienced this in my immediate family. One evening not long after my husband returned to work from paternity leave, he was rushed to the emergency room with the symptoms of a heart attack: sweating, racing heartbeat, shortness of breath, and chest pain. Thankfully, he wasn't having a heart attack, but he was having a major anxiety attack. As we learned, anxiety is a mental illness with several physical symptoms very similar to a heart attack.

When I returned to work when my eight-week maternity leave was over, I was still experiencing postpartum mental health challenges such as insomnia and anxiety. I was too ashamed to tell anyone about the pain I was experiencing as a new mom, feeling both anxious and unable to sleep, and I never asked a doctor for help or received an official diagnosis or treatment. Everyone thought I should be happy to have a beautiful baby, and people joked with me about how new moms never get any sleep. I thought I should be happy too.

The first time I broke the silence about mental illness in the family to our child, he was around eight years old, and we were on our way to church. It was just me and my son in the car. It had been a rough morning back at home. Getting up early and ready for church as a pastor is especially stressful when one's also trying to get the whole family up and ready.

That Sunday morning, my husband was not feeling well enough to get out of bed. It wasn't the flu; it was depression that had him flat on his back. Driving my son to church and me to work, I felt irritated by the inconvenience of depression and frustrated by how it intrudes on our family's life. It steals the energy and joy out of our home. But I knew I had to be patient and compassionate once I arrived at church, thinking of that as part of my job description. I started getting myself into that mindset. Practicing compassion often means saying out loud to myself or others how depression isn't the fault of the person who has it. It's not a character flaw.

I decided it was time to tell our son about mental illness. "Sweetie, Dad's sick today. That's why he's not coming with us to church. It's his brain that isn't feeling well. He has a brain sickness called depression. He gets it a lot. He just doesn't have the energy to get out of bed. He will get better. He just needs to rest. Depression also makes him feel sad. If he doesn't want to spend time with you this afternoon, it's not your fault. It's just part of his sickness. He's had it most of his life."

"Why didn't you tell me sooner?" our son asked.

He was right. I should have had "the talk" with him about the mental illness in our family sooner. Like years before, probably when he was learning his ABCs. That made me wonder: What if we developed ABCs of mental health for our kids to learn?

A is for accept: Accept all your feelings—it's ok to not be ok

B is for believe: Believe in yourself because you are loved

C is for care: Caring for your mental health is important

What would you say for D and E, and the rest of the letters? Think about why you are reading this book and who are the children in our life looking to you for guidance. What would you like children to know about mental health? Remember, we are doing this for the children, for yours and for mine. For our grandchildren and future generations. Take a few minutes and think about what the ABCs of mental health might look like for children to learn. You might be surprised by your inventiveness.

When my husband is having a sick day because of mental illness, he stays in bed. Since I don't live with serious depressive episodes, I don't know what it feels like to be inside his brain. For me, it helps to visualize his illness as a physical illness, even though I cannot see it. So on those sick days of his, I imagine him lying in a hospital bed. I imagine myself sitting beside him and holding his hand until he feels better, I imagine myself being patient and calm and not getting irritated at him for being sick. I repeat these lessons for my son from time to time, and it helps me too; it helps me stay focused on the love in our family, the rainbow behind the cloud.

Since that Sunday morning talk about depression, I've also shared with our child about my own recovery story from complex post-traumatic stress disorder. I shared how talk therapy, going for walks, and giving up alcohol has helped me feel much better.

Today we are all in therapy: couples, family, and individual. It's how we are taking proactive steps to invest in our blessed family's mental well-being.

Getting Help For Yourself

Mental health challenges and illness run in families. Getting our own brains healthy is a critical step in supporting the brain health of our children. Dr. Daniel Siegel says, "As parents become more aware and emotionally healthy, their children reap the rewards and move toward health as well. That means integrating and cultivating your own brain is one of the most loving and generous gifts you can give your children."[49] It's hard to be emotionally available and present with our youth when we ourselves are feeling numb, exhausted, overwhelmed, anxious, and depressed. Yes, the best gift we can give youth is a mentally healthy adult who is emotionally available for them.

Jen, a member of my extended family, shared with me how she navigated helping her child who was struggling with their mental health. She had to get help for herself first. Parenting is hard enough. Having mental health struggles of your own makes parenting even more challenging.

> Being an adult with mental health issues is hard. I have been ashamed of my diagnosis for so long. I didn't want employers to know I had a mental health issue, and I was not an advocate for myself when I should have been. I just felt like I couldn't be open and honest with them, or they would get rid of me.

Jen's experience illustrates the real risks of breaking the silence about mental illness. She had to admit and overcome her own internalized stigma and shame before she could advocate for herself. She was afraid that, if she disclosed her medical condition to her employer, she might lose her job, even though it is illegal to discriminate in this way. People with mental and physical impairments are protected from discrimination under the Americans with Disabilities Act.

With good mental health treatment and medication, Jen was able to overcome the negative experience with her previous employer and is now feeling empowered by the positive experience with her new boss. Jen said, "It hasn't been until the past two years that I opened up to my boss and let her know that I see a psych doctor and that I need to take care of my

---

[49]Daniel Siegel, *The Whole-Brain Child,* 148.

mental health so I can be better at my job. She has been understanding, which is nice."

Taking care of her mental health helped Jen to be a better mom. Now that she knew how to advocate for herself, she was ready to begin advocating for her teenager. Jen's daughter was struggling with anxiety and depression. I asked Jen what helped her to be a better parent to her daughter.

> I think what helped me was that I was trying to teach my daughter that she needed to be her own advocate at school. How could I teach her to do this, and I not follow my same advice? I had to practice what I preached. The more I advocated for her at her school (showing her what she needed to say and do...she has/ had a 504 plan with accommodation for her anxiety/depression) the more I was realizing I could speak up for myself and that it was ok to have these mental health problems and let others know.

Schools provide support to students who have physical and/or mental disabilities and challenges through a formal assessment and planning process that results in an individualized strategy to support the student's education called a 504 plan. In some ways, we parents have got to break the silence about mental illness first ourselves before we can expect to be able to break the silence with others. According to Jen, this can feel like a coming out process.

> The "coming out" part was due to me trying to set an example for my daughter. She was in high school and would be transitioning to college/adulthood soon and she needed to see and know how to advocate for herself. I had to show her how by talking not only about how she should help herself, but also about what worked for me. We had to hold 504 meetings at her school to get accommodations for her, so I was able to talk about myself as well.

Some families experience challenges when it comes to treating mental illness with medication. As parents, we may have had a bad, difficult, or negative experience with medications ourselves in the past and are reluctant to subject our children to the same experience. "The medicine part is a little harder," Jen says.

> I was on medication as a teenager. I didn't think I needed it and would often quit taking it on my own. I then transitioned into adulthood and had kids, but I was not on medication during pregnancy. However, when I was pregnant with my second child, I was very depressed. I wasn't busy at work, and I honestly thought all I was good at was having cute babies.

Experiencing mental health challenges during pregnancy is rough for parents, and navigating treatment can be confusing because of concerns about whether the medication will present risks for the pregnancy. Most doctors now say it's safe for pregnant mothers to stay on their psychiatric meds, but it is still not an easy decision to make.

For Jen, faith was the one thing that helped get her through this valley of the shadow of mental illness while pregnant. She was going to church weekly during that time, and one Sunday the sermon really hit home.

Jen says the sermon she heard was "about what our gifts from God were and how we all had a purpose. For whatever reason this spoke to me. I started thinking more about going back to school. It wasn't until my second baby was six months old that I reapplied to college and started going back and finished."

When Jen, now the mother of three kids, decided to go back to school, she asked her doctor for help managing her mental health.

> I decided I was so tired of being angry and depressed that I went to my primary care doctor and asked to be put back on antidepressants. It felt like the weight was taken off my shoulders and I was feeling better...But over the years...medication needs to be adjusted and changed...I wouldn't change my decision to be put back on medication for anything. I'm a better mother, wife, and educator for it.

Finding purpose and believing your life has meaning is one of the most powerful ways to fight the despair of depression and other mental conditions. For some people like Jen, faith can help connect you to that purpose and meaning.

Blessing Our Families

Supporting and blessing families means improving the quality of mental healthcare for youth and increasing the availability of mental healthcare treatment options. From the mildest symptoms to the most severe symptoms of mental illness, children and families deserve access to the best and most affordable care possible. Families also need support from the wider community as they navigate how best to care for the mental health issues.

My friend Rev. Lizzy is a mom and a minister who lives with serious mental illness. She is a children's hospital chaplain and her ministry is with youth who have mental illness. Lizzy shocked herself one day when she called upon her community for help that would save her life. Lizzy broke her silence on social media about her bipolar mental illness and thoughts of suicide by asking for donations to help her pay for intensive inpatient treatment.

In response to Lizzy's request for support, within forty-eight hours, her wider community raised over $15,000 to support her and her family, including her five children, so that she could get the mental health care she needed. Lizzy was blessed by the community because of her courage to ask for help. Lizzy's life was saved by the community's generous outpouring of love.

Lizzy gave me permission to share her letter, saying, "There is freedom in saying, 'this is what I've gone through, who I am, and what has helped me make it to this point.'"

Below is Lizzy's heartfelt letter to her community, telling her personal story of a long and difficult struggle with mental illness. She then requested assistance from the community to help her get better.

Lizzy testifies to the life-saving power of breaking the silence:

> Ten years ago, I found myself at rock bottom. After a series of inpatient psychiatric admissions, I was court-ordered to a state psychiatric facility. Unable to work. Unable to be with my husband or care for our son.

> I was discharged in July of 2011. I immediately sought out the dialectical behavior therapy program that had been recommended to me. I completed that program, and it changed my life.

> Over the course of the next ten years, we added four more children to our family. We moved so I could attend seminary. Three years later, I graduated summa cum laude with my Master of Divinity degree. I found my sacred vocational calling of providing spiritual care for children and teens experiencing mental illness—after all, I understand the pain of trauma/grief/depression in my soul.

> Now, I have the spiritual grounding, knowledge, and experience to provide spiritual care that helps kids and teens develop spiritual strength and begin to address spiritual struggles. I'm good at this work. And for the past five years, I have worked with hundreds of kiddos individually and in spirituality groups. This is my honor and my joy.

> While I experienced struggles here and there over the past decade, I felt free…I thought I had mostly left my mental illness in past. Then, in August of 2020, I found myself descending into the depths. I knew where this path could lead, so I had blood work done and began taking vitamins to make up for some deficiencies

the doctor found. I found a therapist and saw her weekly. And I got worse.

I began to wish that I wouldn't wake up. When my turmoil became unbearable, I began planning to end my life. My friend got me to the hospital in the nick of time in March of 2021. The care I received was compassionate, and their aftercare was impressive. At discharge, I still suffered horribly but had some hope in my heart that I had turned the tide.

I returned home to my family. I began taking medication prescribed by a psychiatrist I deeply trust. I began receiving esketamine treatments (a nasal spray for treatment-resistant depression), twice per week. I attended a partial hospitalization program. I returned to work. And still, I felt worse and worse.

I returned to the hospital last week, cared for by the same treatment team. My nurse practitioner, a woman of wisdom and compassion, strongly recommended residential treatment. She felt it might save my life. "You've tried everything else," she told me. "This is something you haven't done before, and it might make the difference." My husband and friends are on board to hold down the fort at home so I can receive this care.

The residential facility I've chosen provides care for women who have experienced trauma and have mood disorders—women like me. I would have a month to live and focus on myself and my treatment. Like dialectical behavior therapy did in 2011, I am hoping this program provides support and care that gives me ten more years of stability, joy, and purpose. Or, God willing, even more than that.

I would miss the kids terribly and worry about leaving my job even for this brief time. Would it be worth it to save my life so I can spend the next decades loving them well? It is the financial costs that feel insurmountable. I'm hoping you might help with that. The facility I hope to go to does accept and work with our insurance, but it is out of network. They don't offer financing, and the money is due upfront.

For me to do this, we need $15,000. We can put some on a CareCredit card, but not everything…I'm hoping to leave in the next two weeks, but I have to pay first.

I am scared, hopeful, and committed to getting well. I want to return to work, ready to care for the vulnerable, courageous kids

I support every day. Most importantly, our five children need me, and I desperately want to be with them as they grow up.

This may be the hardest thing I have ever done, and your support provides the strength to keep trying. I feel your hope for me, even as I struggle to feel hope for myself.

Lizzy's courage in breaking the silence made it possible for people to be invited to help support her and her blessed family. It's important to hear stories like the story Lizzy shares because this type of struggle is all too common. What is less common is the ability to ask for this kind of significant support. How beautiful is it that she was able to ask for help and that she got it. What if more people felt as if they could ask for help? What if they could feel hopeful and assured that their needs would be met?

I followed up with Lizzy after she come back home from the residential treatment center. She says that it saved her life but it didn't cure her from mental illness. She told me she "identified as someone who made it out of hell—and thought I'd be mostly ok forever. I felt like it feels like a blow to be struggling so much now, even though I know I haven't done anything to deserve this." The ongoing nature of her chromic mental illness makes it especially challenging.

Lizzy said, "Some weeks are pretty good. Last week, depression and anxiety overwhelmed me, stealing from me even the idea that a meaningful life was a remote possibility." For Lizzy, her bipolar disorder can remove any pleasure from life.

"The fog on the lake didn't move me—it wasn't beautiful at all."

"The frappé I drank tasted like nothing."

"Existing felt painful."

But then, life slowly returned. Lizzy says, "By Sunday, I felt like myself again. Connection, joy, meaning, and pleasure were within easy reach."

Lizzy's life is a testimony of the power of creating a support network. She says, "I am blessed beyond measure by a support system that almost literally holds me together. And thankfully, I am home, alive, and able to continue this life of parenting, being a wife/friend/etc., and doing ministry. I work hard to care for myself and to be cared for, and that helps for sure."

Lizzy's story shows us that the hardest part of mental illness is how isolating it can be and how we think we are the only ones who struggle. By sharing our stories in the open, we can show how we made it through the valley of the shadow of mental illness, even if only for a short time. These stories offer hope.

Lizzy says, "I would do almost anything to never feel lost in such darkness again, and—I'm not sure that anything other than these struggles could have enabled me to let myself be held and loved so tenderly. Interdependence doesn't come easily to me, but I keep getting chances to try it out."

I asked Lizzy what she has learned about mental health that she would want readers to know, and she said, "I have learned that mental health isn't an achievement or guaranteed for those who do self-care, therapy, and take meds. We can do all the things and still feel depressed—still suffer. And we are as worthy of love and meaning when we are depressed as we are when depression has slunk back into the hell where it came from."

Hell is not a physical place, but the feeling of suffering from mental illness alone and without hope. We can help people get out of this mental hell, as Lizzy calls it, by witnessing their suffering and loving them through their suffering. We can hold their testimony and bear witness to their stories and pain. They and we don't have to suffer alone. Sometimes the best thing we can do to help is to listen.

To break the silence about mental illness and ask for help is hard. For people without mental illness, it seems simple—just ask for help! But the stigma and shame of mental illness, plus the physical symptoms of fatigue and brain fog often make it physically impossible to ask for help. The people most in need of help often are not able to ask for it.

For that reason, it's up to us to be on the lookout for those who need help but can't ask for it, for whatever reason, whether it's a child, teen, or an adult. Mental illness is not a private affair that people should have to deal with alone in hopes it will get better on its own. Mental illness is a disease that requires the community's help.

One way of getting there is to begin to talk with others about our own mental health more freely and honestly—before we are in crisis mode and no longer have the capacity to do so. We talk about our physical health often enough—our diabetes, hypertension, asthma, heart disease, and cancer. Now it's time to normalize talking about our mental health too. By talking about it, we'll chip away at the fear of discrimination, stigma, and shame that keeps us silent and gets in the way of treatment, care, support, and recovery.

It turns out that blessed families need an entire network of care from several community institutions: medical, faith, and educational. We want our medical safety net to be more robust and inclusive of mental health. However, even if all the political and policy stars aligned and created the strongest medical safety net possible, it would still be incomplete without the vital connections of our school and faith communities. The good news is that when these institutions work together across disciplines, we can help our children thrive and enjoy their childhoods. There is hope for families and children living with mental health challenges.

Blessed families are like patchwork quilts. Above my desk at home where I work and write is a framed quilt square my mother gave to me and others in my family. This and other quilt squares are from a patchwork quilt my great-great-grandmother Ella Priscilla McElhaney (1860–1951) hand-stitched together. My mother attached this story to the back of each quilt square.

> This handmade quilt was pieced together and quilted in the late 1940s by Ella Priscilla for her great-granddaughter Jennie Murrell Wilson [my mother]. Jennie was five years old and just recovering from spinal meningitis, which at the time was often fatal. The quilt was made from dresses, shirts, and scraps from clothes worn pre-World War II. The quilt had 12 original squares, and this is one of them. We hope you will pass this heirloom Quilt Block on to a family member who will also treasure it...This Quilt Block is given to you in loving memory of family who died in 2020. Children of Katie Pearl McElhaney Hayes: Beulah Mae Hayes Wilson (1921–2020) and Billy Joe Hayes (1934–2020) and the Great, Great, Great Granddaughter of Ella Priscilla McElhaney, Sydney Elise Griffith (2004–2020).

The quilt square is a reminder that our families are sewn together piece-by-piece, stitch-by-stitch. Our stories are connected, stitched together by time, DNA, events, and the home we share. Families are like patchwork quilts reminding us that we are part of a greater whole and we all have a story to tell.

Blessed are the families, for within them we can tell our stories and break the generations of silence about mental illness.

5

Blessed Schools

One day while working on this chapter I saw a female hawk land on the limb of a sycamore tree about ten feet away outside my third-floor window where I sit at my writing desk. The hawk turned her head and our eyes connected as she stared right at me. I looked at her and wondered how she took care of her young and if there was anything our families, schools, and faith communities might learn from her parenting.

Hawks have one to five babies per brood. When the babies hatch, they are helpless, tiny, and unable to lift their heads. Mother hawks aggressively defend their children, keeping them safe and alive at all costs.[50]

When it comes to youth and mental health, our schools can be like the mother hawk, keeping our children safe, cared for, and alive. Now imagine:

- What if that safe shelter became a more proactive form of protection?
- What if schools became places that defended our children from risk factors of mental illness?
- What if schools became places where teens were regularly screened for mental health concerns?
- What if schools became the places where our children learned about mental health and learned the warning signs of mental illness?
- What if schools became the places where our children accessed quality and free mental health services such as talk therapy and peer support groups? Advocating for in-school mental health education and support services is part of a growing movement, yet there is some resistance from parents concerned about preserving individual rights. Is mental health education and support also a right for all children?

Providing Safe Environments

I come from a family of educators. My mother taught at public schools for over four decades as a kindergarten teacher to low-income students. I know how important it was to my mother that her students felt safe,

[50]"Red-tailed Hawk: Life History," All About Birds, https://www.allaboutbirds.org/guide/Red-tailed_Hawk/lifehistory.

respected, and loved in her classroom. When I was a kid growing up in the 1980s, some parents did fear for their students at school. But their worries mostly had to do with poverty and violence in the neighborhoods surrounding the schools, and sadly, that didn't make news. Today we all worry about our schools not being safe because of mass shootings. Ever since the mass shootings at Columbine High School in 1999, and at Sandy Hook Elementary in 2012, and the many in between those dates and since, schools across America have invested millions of taxpayer dollars into security measures to help prevent more mass shootings. What would it look like for our schools to make investments to prevent and treat mental health challenges and receive equal funding for a counselor, nurse, school psychologist, or social worker?

According to the Report of the Federal Commission on School Safety from 2018,

> Many schools lack the capacity to identify and adequately treat mental illness. School principals report that student mental health needs are one of their biggest challenges. Integrating mental health prevention and treatment services and supports into schools can provide many benefits, including reducing risk for mental health disorders and increasing access to care for those who need treatment while reducing the stigma of seeking help. It can also help provide early identification, intervention, and a full continuum of services while using a multidisciplinary approach. This involves engaging teachers, parents, and community providers as partners in promoting social, emotional, and academic learning for all students.[51]

I'm convinced that the best way to keep our children safe is to invest in prevention of mental illness. We do that by investing in mental health. What would it look like if we invested in the mental well-being of our children by staffing the schools with mental health professionals? What if schools integrated mental health education into the K-12 curriculum? What if schools supported peer-led mental health clubs to develop leadership and advocacy skills for youth?

School Mental Health Professionals

One significant way we can bring affordable, quality, and accessible mental health care to youth is by staffing our schools with mental health professionals. According to the 2019 ACLU report *Cops and No Counselors:*

---

[51] *Report of the Federal Commission on School Safety*, U.S. Department of Education, January 18, 2018, under review as of December 9, 2021, https://www2.ed.gov/documents/school-safety/school-safety-report.pdf.

How the Lack of School Mental Health Staff is Harming Students, "school counselors, nurses, social workers, and psychologists are frequently the first to see children who are sick, stressed, traumatized, may act out, or may hurt themselves or others."[52]

Schools that provide mental health providers see the benefits in improved attendance rates, lower rates of suspension and other disciplinary incidents, expulsion, and improved academic achievement, career preparation, and graduation rates. Mental health providers in the school also improve school safety. In a statement to the Federal Commission on School Safety, Dr. Laura Hodges, a Nationally Certified School Counselor, said, "We must arm school counselors across the country with the appropriate counselor to student ratio (1 to 250). School counselors, social workers, and school psychologists are all on the mental health frontlines."[53] Only three states meet the recommended student-to-counselor ratio.

Mental Health Awareness and Leadership Development Clubs in Schools

I first met Doug Beach at a national gathering of faith leaders who gathered in Washington, D.C. to consult with the US Administration about mental health. Doug's passion for supporting families through mental health crises was evident as he talked about the support groups he nurtured through his role with National Alliance on Mental Illness (NAMI). He and I stayed in touch and began working together on the board for the interfaith mental health ministry Pathways to Promise.

In the fall of 2020, I again had occasion to meet up with Doug, this time in San Antonio, where he serves as President of NAMI San Antonio. Only I wasn't there for business. It was the day after Sydney died and I was meeting with family. When my flight landed, I called Doug from the terminal's gate. I was distraught, sleep-deprived, and navigating my own anxiety, since I was traveling during the pandemic before the vaccine.

Doug took my call and listened to my heartache. He met my family for lunch and connected us to emergency mental health support to help us process the grief and trauma as a family. He was there for us in our time of need and he was our angel. When I thanked Doug for his generous, kind, and compassionate support, he said, "When my family was going through a difficult time, angels were there for us. That's just what we do."

---

[52]Amir Whitaker et al., *Cops and No Counselors: How the Lack of Mental Health Staff is Harming Students*, American Civil Liberties Union, 2019, https://www.aclu.org/report/cops-and-no-counselors.

[53]Ibid.

With NAMI San Antonio, Doug is leading a new effort to collaborate with the school district to bring mental health clubs to schools. The idea of mental health clubs in schools was conceived by Donnie Whited, another member of the NAMI San Antonio board. Her idea was born from decades of experience in schools teaching at-risk middle and high school students.

As an educator, Donnie saw youth often coming from traumatic and terrible home situations, exhibiting behavioral problems in class. They did not get the care, attention, and help they needed. Too often we expect students to go to class acting as if nothing is happening in their home and family lives to hinder their learning. Donnie looked closer at these youth, saw beyond the classroom to the root cause of the behavioral problems, and thought that starting mental health clubs in the high school might be a solution, or at least a helpful support.

Donnie says that youth seek positive connections in schools and desire schools to be more attentive when it comes to their mental health needs. They want to be in an informal peer support group rather than a clinical setting. Youth want education and information about mental health to help reduce stigma and give them a pathway to manage their own health. Students say they want a club to share their feelings so they "won't look like outcasts." Students want to be leaders and want to create clubs that are open and inclusive to all.

One challenge working within a standard school day is that classes and activities are scheduled and prescribed. There's no extra room or space in the curriculum for helping students cope or deal with mental health challenges. For example, a Texas school counselor said "At 7am, I have to be on playground to supervise, then at 8am I have to be a hall monitor, and so on. I didn't have anything to do with meeting with students or helping them deal with mental health issues." And this is in Texas, where legislation has passed to provide extra counselors in schools.

Despite Texas laws, working through a school system is challenging and barriers to accessing resources still exist. From this frustrating experience, the idea of a mental health extracurricular activity was born. The vision for mental health clubs is to meet for an hour once a month and share an activity outside of school. While the club is facilitated by a school counselor, it is led and run by the students who decide what the club will focus on.

NAMI recommends that clubs provide three classes: (1) on ACEs, (2) companionship training for youth, and (3) suicide prevention. NAMI will also provide an "Ending the Silence" presentation with a young person—a peer, another student talking about their life experience—telling their story on how they dealt with mental illness and where they are today.

Doug said leaders in one Texas school district he approached quickly acknowledged the huge need for mental health support and admitted they could not meet it without outside support from groups like NAMI. They supported the idea of grass roots, student led mental health clubs and during 2021 the clubs have taken off like wildfire in the district. Doug explained the rapid uptake by noting it's the students who know when they may have a mental health issue and are aware if a friend or family member is struggling. The clubs are helping to remove the stigma and offer a safe place for students to talk about mental illness. The leaders in the district have expressed a desire to have mental health clubs established in all high schools, middle schools, and elementary schools in the district by the end of 2022.

In a recent conversation about the school mental health club model Doug said:

> Now is the opportunity. That's what this is…We are at this time in history where there's such a heightened degree of awareness of mental health and the lack of resources is overwhelming. What do you do? You have to get the community together. You have to get something we are all working on, getting out of our silos, and figure out how to do this together. We can work in nontraditional ways with people we may not have worked with in the past, but now we have the same goal: healthy communities.

School Mental Health Chaplains

What if schools invested in providing interfaith chaplains? While there would likely be disagreement in some communities over whether school chaplains represent the state or a religion (or endorsement of one religion over another), there are as many arguments—and perhaps more—to be made for the benefits. There is a movement focusing on the importance of these roles at the intersection of spiritual and mental health, particularly in times of grief. I learned from Rev. Rachel Frey is a ministry colleague of mine who works as a chaplain for a window manufacturing company in Canada. The model of chaplaincy, long established in the healthcare sector, is growing in popularity in the business sector. Why not in the educational community too? I've already seen a model of how this can work. Her role is to walk around the workspace and check in on the employees, simply asking how they are doing and then listening. She can provide them resources if they need additional emotional support.

The chaplain model could be supportive not only to students but to staff as well. Many helping professionals are overworked and underpaid, with caseloads much higher than in any other setting, making it difficult to provide care in ways that they would like. Perhaps it's time to think about schools the same way we think about hospital systems and businesses and consider the benefit of providing culturally sensitive spiritual care to those who inhabit those spaces.

Mental Health and Students of Color

The Mental Health America report says that in 2019 only half of the White youth who needed mental health care received services.[54] The barriers to access are even worse for youth of color, with only about a third of Black and Hispanic youth who needed care receiving mental health services.[55] How can we bridge this gap and address racial inequality?

The Mental Health America report findings show that youth of color are more likely than White youth to receive mental health services in school as opposed to a doctor's office.[56] This means that schools can be the mother hawk for our children's mental health, especially when they connect our children of color to accessible and affordable services. Having mental health care available in the schools removes the need for health insurance and transportation, two of the most common barriers for youth of color when receiving mental health care services.

Counseling support services in the school put professionals in the right place, at the right time, and without any direct cost to the child or family in need. Such a model promotes equity and reduces disparities in access to mental health care. Blessing our youth in schools with on-site mental health resources is a win-win for everyone.

Senti-Mental

My niece Sydney didn't get the support she needed from her high school. She had reached out to her school guidance counselor multiple times, calling and leaving voice messages and never hearing anything back. This lack of availability and access to mental health support at school inspired what turned out to be Sydney's final school project during the spring before she died by suicide.

That project was to create a design for a new nonprofit, a school-based mental health education program that would be called "Senti-Mental." Sydney wrote this in her school paper:

> Senti-Mental is a service for the good of the general public. Our dedicated team is made up of passionate volunteers and

[54]"Mental Health America Report."
[55]Ibid.
[56]Ibid.

professional, highly educated mental health providers who are always willing to put forth the time and effort to ensure that our audience is receiving the most accurate and beneficial information regarding mental health and those who struggle with it.

My project is in the business of educating, plain and simple. Our goal is to make as many people aware of the updated and most essential mental health information, with special care towards breaking the stigma surrounding this previously taboo topic.

As many know, nonprofits tend to need good-hearted philanthropists to make their goal possible, and Senti-Mental is no exception. Considering that the science of mental health is at an all-time high and today's youth is increasingly aware, but not properly educated, about mental health issues through the media, I would argue that my project is one of the more prominent education-based nonprofits that needs funding.

The maximum potential of my project will be reached through individual presentations and eventually an online platform. The cost for this project should be minimal, considering it is comprised of volunteers. Since the presentations would be done with the classroom equipment that is already there, the only foreseeable costs are for recording equipment, website design, and possibly social media advertisement once the project reaches that level.

I have read and reread Sydney's proposal dozens of times. I keep looking for clues. I keep looking for answers. Every time I reread her idea for Senti-Mental I think, "She really knew what she was talking about."

After Sydney's suicide, her father reflected on what he can do now to help ensure that what happened to Sydney doesn't happen to any other kid. He said the school has a critical role to play and he had an idea to share. In an email he told me,

> I am in the process of writing to Sydney's school to let them know the impact that a dramatic drop in grades may have on high-achieving perfectionistic children. She was seventh in her class with near perfect grades. She was taking six AP classes and struggling. The last activity we can see on the day she died was her accessing her grades; she had failed chemistry and physics.

Sydney's father continued by saying he wanted to suggest a change in the way failing grades are communicated to students.

> I want to model my suggestion after the CDC's recommendation on how newly diagnosed HIV positive test results should be delivered: the best practice is to convey an HIV test result face-

to-face. This provides for the appropriate support, education, and resources that these patients require after receiving the devastating news. Likewise, I think the school's online learning platform should not release failing grades to students who are at home alone when reading the news for the first time. Rather, there could be an asterisk, or some kind of notation that a Parent-Teacher conference with the child is required. This would protect the adolescent who is a high-achieving, anxious, and depressed perfectionist. This is because, 'setbacks or failures, either real or imagined, can sometimes precipitate suicide' (p. 90, *Night Falls Fast*, by Kay Redfield Jamison[57]). Again, a computer algorithm put in place on schoology.com could have saved my daughter's life.

Schools can help save lives by listening to their own students and families within their school community. What if Sydney's school had taken steps toward partnering with mental health educators, as she proposed in her project? On a more basic level, what if they had simply followed up when she reached out to the guidance counselor for help? What forward-looking lessons can school administrators, families, education app developers, and other advocates learn from Sydney's death about how we communicate difficult news, such as failing grades, in school?

Sydney was an adventurous, smart, and talented young woman. I want her to be remembered as a young woman with a plan to help other students. Sydney always thought of others first and she wanted to help other students because she knew firsthand the kinds of struggles youth faced in school and at home. Many school staff, teachers, and administrators who see strong students like Sydney suddenly struggling are often too overwhelmed and under-resourced to help connect students to support services. Let's work together to fix this problem. How many more students will die because their well-articulated pleas for help are ignored, dismissed, or downplayed by an overwhelmed and underfunded school system—let alone those students who can't muster reaching out for help?

The report by Mental Health America emphasizes that empowering kids like Sydney is a key strategy for being responsive to the immediate needs of young people. Our youth know what interventions they need *right now* to improve their mental health and well-being. Sydney knew what kind of help she needed. The children are telling us. Are we listening?

Blessing Our Youth at School

Central to empowering youth is creating intentional spaces where they can talk openly and honestly about their needs and where it is ok to ask

[57]Kay Redfield Jamison, *Night Falls Fast: Understanding Suicide* (New York: Alfred A. Knopf, 1999).

for help. Then, when the youth tell us what they want and need, it is our responsibility to listen. Imagine how powerful it would be to empower youth to tell us how they want to see the problems solved and how they can play a key role in those solutions.

The Mental Health America report findings indicate that youth are most likely to talk to a friend when experiencing mental health symptoms. Some schools, as we heard earlier from Doug in San Antonio, beginning to offer peer support programs, which allow for early conversations and access to support for students from diverse backgrounds. Such peer connections are critical resources for children and teens.

Imagine what it would be if in the amount of time it takes to recite the Pledge of Allegiance every youth in America's schools completed a simple, daily mental health electronic screening that could alert adults if they needed additional care and support. Since the pandemic, children and teens are already using school issued computer devices. Some class activities even incorporate the use of students' personal smartphones. What if we could install an app that would track a student's daily mental health, noting changes and especially alerting adults to thoughts of self-harm? On a scale of one to five, students could let us know how they feel that morning as the school day begins.

5: **Great**

4: **Good**

3: **Ok**

2: **Not good**

1: **Not safe**

Then, all the students reporting a two or a one would get a follow-up notification inviting them to talk to a school nurse, social worker, or mental health professional. There might also be a peer group available for students who are struggling that day or need additional attention or assistance. The group could meet daily, be held over lunch and led by a trained adult facilitator.

Students are eager to learn more about mental health conditions. They want to know the early warning signs of someone who might be suicidal and what to say to them and how to help. They want to learn methods of coping with stress, depression, and anxiety, and hear from peers who have had the same experiences with living with mental illness and coping in recovery.

Schools are part of an eco-system of care and are integral to the mental health of our youth. Schools can be compared to a mother hawk in a nest, providing a safe environment where the young can grow, learn, and prepare to take flight out into the world.

By working together as a community, educators, mental health professionals, families, and students, we can bless our youth and save lives.

Blessed are the schools, for within the school community we can empower our youth to take flight, soaring into the future with strength and hope.

6

Blessed Faith

How can faith play an important role in our blessed youth's lives? Faith traditions, faith communities, and spiritual practices can be the thin golden thread that helps us hold onto hope.

After her death Sydney's father reflected, "I keep getting the feeling that God is trying to reach me." A friend reached out to him, inviting him to join a men's Bible study. Sydney's father responded saying, God is "using you to be His hands and feet. For that I am grateful, and I am listening. I want to thank you, the way you showed up immediately at my doorstep that awful November morning, the way you were present with us and prayed with us. That was unforgettable, and if it weren't for that, I may have rejected God forever."

People of faith show up for each other during times of need. What might have happened if no one had reached out and shown up at the doorstep for Sydney's father when his heart was breaking with the news of his teenage daughter's suicide? People of faith show up regularly to bring comfort in times of despair, tragedy, and loss. People in faith communities understand that sometimes we need another person to believe for us until we can believe for ourselves again. When we are in the shadows of pain, we need someone to come alongside us, hold us up, and carry a candle of hope on our behalf.

Faith can fill the void we experience in life when our deepest longings to be known and loved are unmet. As a child growing up in a home where there was serious chronic and untreated mental illness, I was blessed to be part of a faith community that made me feel loved. As a young child, I experienced church as a safe place where I could receive comfort, reassurance, and be invited to trust in God's love for me.

My ancestry includes mainly German, Welsh, and English folks. In these ethnic cultures, it's not common to show lots of physical affection. In my family this held true. We did not verbalize love for one another, nor were we "warm and fuzzy." I do not have a single memory of my father holding, hugging, or touching me growing up. What I remember is asking my mother to rub my back to help me fall asleep at night. She was always happy to do so, but I wonder if the thought would have occurred to her if I hadn't asked.

When I went to church as a little girl, the Lutheran minister would invite us all up to the altar for holy communion. In turn he would place his large and strong hand gently upon my bowed head for a blessing. This touch meant the world to me. I was like a hug from God. That tender touch was sacred, not because it came from the pastor or because it happened in church, but because it was one of the only intentionally affirming touches I remember as a young child.

When I baptize infants, I hold them close to my heart and gently bless their foreheads with water that the congregation and I have prayed over. The water is made holy by our collective love. This is a ritual of sacred touch, using water that affirms their worth, their membership in the human family, and that says, "You belong here. You are loved."

In the sacrament of holy communion, we come together to share bread and wine (or juice) in symbolic unity and affirm our care for one another and God's care for us. These sacraments of the faith are gifts that support mental well-being and offer spiritual healing to people when they are feeling lonely, disconnected, and unloved.

We can use institutions—such as our schools and churches—to bless our young people's mental health in a variety of ways, several of which I mentioned in Chapter 5. First, we can use them to create educational opportunities. Second, we can facilitate connections to accessible, affordable, and quality community mental health care. Third, through our institutions we can provide empowerment training in self-advocacy (ways for people to find their voices and tell their stories). Fourth, we can create spaces for peer support. And fifth, we can create mentoring opportunities.

Building Trust

Faith communities can create places of belonging and trust for children, youth, and families. Mental health flourishes and thrives in caring and compassionate communities. At a time when many churches are asking themselves what happened to all the children and families, Christian educator and minister Lee Yates says we need to go outside of the church and find them where they are and listen to them. Lee says, "We need to build relationships with the children, youth, and families around us with no goal of membership or institutional involvement. No strings attached!"[58]

---

[58]Lee Yates, "Breaking News: Relationships Matter!" *Vital Signs & Statistics* (blog), *The Center for Analytics, Research & Development, and Data for the United Church of Christ*, July 26, 2021, https://carducc.wordpress.com/2021/07/26/breaking-news-relationships-matter/.

In 2021, the United Church of Christ Mental Health Network co-created a resource called "Are We Listening: Trauma and Youth Resources." The free resource is an hour-long webinar to inform and educate faith communities. Included are suggestions for creating a trauma-informed youth ministry. Other key topics include how faith communities can minimize triggers, ensuring physical needs are being met, create routine, and create peace rooms and restorative justice circles. The webinar also includes information on how to offer brain breaks, mindfulness practices/breathing, continued staff training, support teams and communities of care, and sanctuary.[59]

Spiritual Care and Suicide

Because I am a pastor, I think a lot about how faith communities can be a blessing for children, teens, and families experiencing mental illness. My own family often looks to me for spiritual guidance, for prayer at special occasions, and to officiate at weddings, baptisms, and funerals. When Sydney died by suicide, I had the heartbreaking honor of writing her obituary and collecting stories from family and friends about her life. Here is what I wrote for Sydney's obituary.

> Sydney was a free spirit who always loved adventure including scuba diving, world travel, skateboarding, snowboarding, and most recently taking flight lessons. Sydney was a gifted musician who played several instruments including the acoustic guitar, electric guitar, ukulele, violin, drums, and cello. Sydney was gifted, kind, inquisitive, thoughtful, and a bright star in our orbit.
>
> Sydney was adored by her extended family including cousins, aunts, uncles, and grandparents. Sydney's life will be remembered as one of wonderment and awe for her brilliance and beauty and her care for all of creation.

You can see from reading the obituary that in our initial grief we were not ready to name publicly the cause of Sydney's death. Long before her death, I had learned and internalized that suicide needs to be named as the cause of death to help reduce stigma. Yet some families, including my own, are not ready to name the cause of death when it is suicide, especially immediately following the death.

My family's experience taught me nothing really makes sense in the aftermath of a child's suicide because our pain is too raw and our minds too clouded and blank to field questions. Now, looking back, our family cannot remember what even happened for the Thanksgiving and Christmas holidays just weeks after her death. We were in so much shock and intense pain.

[59]"Trauma & Youth Resources," United Church of Christ Mental Health Network, https://www.mhn-ucc.org/trauma-and-youth-resources/.

One of the best things we can do in the immediate aftermath of suicide is to be present. Being fully present is a spiritual practice. There are no magic words that can be said to make the loss hurt less. What is healing is being together. No one should be left alone to hold this kind of grief.

I remember holding baby Sydney in my arms when I baptized her. As part of the baptism ceremony, I read Psalm 23 and led the family in reciting the Lord's Prayer. In baptism we celebrate the gift of life, affirm its beauty and value, and promise to nurture its flourishing. In baptism we remind ourselves of God's love for us and that God's Spirit is forever with us. The religious ritual of baptism is important to Christians because it is a visible sign of an inward and invisible grace. When I baptized Sydney, I made the sign of the cross on her tiny forehead. Holy water, blessed by sacred words, touched her delicate infant skin.

We claimed this sweet baby as made in God's image. We claimed her life as sacred. We claimed her as God's gift to the world. Her life will always be sacred, even in death. She remains and forever will remain a treasured gift from God. Suicide is not a sin or a curse or a punishment from God. Sydney was loved by God and remains loved by God.

I never would have imagined that sixteen years after her baptism our family would be gathered for her funeral. Standing beneath a large wooden cross in church and beside a rose salt stone urn that held her ashes, I read scripture for Sydney's memorial service. My voice quivered with emotion. Once again, I proclaimed God's love for us and that God's Spirit is forever with us. I celebrated the beauty and value of Sydney's life. I read Psalm 23 and led the family in reciting the Lord's Prayer. In death, as in life, we can turn to spirituality for comfort and hope. Suicide does not erase the importance, value, beauty, and influence of a life.

Sitting With One Another in God's Love

One of the most important lessons of faith we can teach our children is that they are loved unconditionally and beyond our wildest imagination by God, the universe, a higher power, or by whatever name we choose to use. This divine, universal love is with them, inside of them, and goes with them, no matter who they are or where they are on life's journey, and no matter the state of their mental health.

Mental health challenges affect our sense of self-worth and our self-esteem. They can make us feel unworthy, unwanted, and unlovable. One way to support positive mental health is therefore through connection to a faith tradition and faith communities that mirrors back to us our own belovedness as children of God.

Faith communities can integrate mental health education, advocacy, and support into their mission and ministries. When faith communities make a commitment to supporting mental health, they offer unconditional positive regard and celebrate the value of every person. Each person is loved and each person matters to God no matter what.

Working with the UCC Mental Health Network I helped to develop a mental health ministry guide. We created a simple-to-follow process to help congregations become Welcoming, Inclusive, Supportive, and Engaged (WISE) for mental health. This process includes educating staff and members of the congregation through programs like Mental Health First Aid, teaching adult and youth education classes about mental health, and preaching about mental illness from the pulpit.

As I consult with congregations across the country about mental health, I find that the most powerful mental health ministries are born from members of the congregation themselves breaking the silence about mental illness, family, and faith. Listening to people's stories of their struggles, their challenges, and how they survived creates spaces for other people to begin to connect and share their stories.

Pastors are often the first ones to hear the intimate stories of personal struggle. Yet telling the pastor is not enough. In addition, we can provide more support by forming faith communities where trust is established through shared experiences and stories of challenges and victories can be shared. In the absence of such trust, suffering people can feel isolated and alone and lives can quickly fall apart.

I'll never forget visiting one church where I was invited to preach. After the service, a young family approached me to express their gratitude for my words about mental health and the important role faith communities play in offering support to families. They shared their child had been recently diagnosed with multiple mental health challenges. The parents were overwhelmed by the complex diagnosis and challenges they faced and needed support. They hadn't talked with anyone at the church and were at a loss regarding where to go or to whom they could talk about it. No less than fifteen minutes later, a second young family came up to me and shared almost an identical story, echoing the feeling of being overwhelmed, the lack of support, and not knowing to whom they should talk. They likewise had not told anyone at church about their situation, not the senior pastor nor the youth and family pastor.

This is an all too common story unfolding in faith communities everywhere. The stigma and shame parents feel creates an invisible barrier to talking about one's family's struggles with mental illness. Before I left that Sunday, I spoke to the pastors and encouraged them to think about creating an opportunity for families to connect for support, and to explore starting a mental health ministry. I hold the stories of these families in my heart.

The good news is there are more and more faith communities sponsoring spiritual support groups. These groups bring people together, helping them feel less alone and assisting them in breaking the silence about mental illness. These weekly gatherings are not meant to replace professional mental health care, but instead to provide spiritual care and support.

I colead the spiritual support group for mental health at First Congregational United Church of Christ, where I serve as pastor. The hour we spend together each week, online or in person, begins with a brief sacred reading, such as a psalm or poem. Then time is open for anyone who wants to share a reflection on the reading or check in about how they are doing.

We listen without judgment and sometimes we sit in silence, honoring the power of simply being together in the presence of God and a supportive community. Lastly, we close our time together with prayer.

As a spiritual support group, we promise to keep the stories confidential, and we don't offer advice. We provide peer support and compassionate listening. In fact, the group itself is designed to be led by lay people. Rather than relying on mental health professionals, it relies on the power of speaking and hearing one another's stories and testimonies.

Many different kinds of people are drawn to this group. Some of us live with mental health challenges. Some of us are parents of children with mental illness. Some of us are the spouse of a partner with brain disorders. Some of us have grandchildren with mental health challenges.

No matter who is coming to the support group or why they are coming, each time we feel better having spent the time together. There are few places in the world today where we can show up fully as we are, our whole selves, unedited, seen and heard without judgment or shame. Spiritual healing comes when we can tell the true stories of our struggles and pain. This is part of mental health too.

First Church Berkeley United Church of Christ in California is also a WISE church for mental health. The Rev. Molly Baskette serves as its senior minister. Judy, a church member, helps to lead the mental health ministry. She is a retired nurse and the mother of a child with schizophrenia, a serious and chronic lifelong, mental illness. Based on her professional and personal experiences, Judy knows first-hand that families living with mental health challenges need support and that faith communities can be a blessing for children, teens, and families.

One of the best ways to engage and interest others in a topic like mental health ministry is to tell our personal stories and experiences. During the early phases of forming this mental health ministry, Judy shared her powerful testimony with the congregation. Testimonies are shared stories that have a way of touching people deeply and help others begin to see and feel the deep pain people are silently holding inside. Here is Judy's testimony in her own words:

> Mental illness came into my life over thirty years ago and has been present with me every day since then. It caused me to rethink my preconceptions of what mental illness is and how to live with it. While I am not here to talk about my mentally ill family member, I want to share with you what this journey has been like for me.

> Concerns started slowly, like little ripples in a pond. Small issues and red flags were constant and only grew, despite my best efforts to try to control them and make things right. Over time these ripples became daily waves. My efforts to direct things and set limits only made everything worse.

> Eventually mental illness caused a tsunami. I experienced sleepless nights, stomach upsets, and constant worry. I would try to bolster myself up, resolve to make things better, only to be taken down by daily life. My resolve would get me nowhere.

> Mental illness became bigger than we could handle in our own home. We realized we needed help and started reaching out. Over the years we received many services. However, there was no doubt that mental illness was here to stay. At the same time, I was relieved that I could put a name to it and accept that the problem was bigger than we could manage.

> And where was the church during these years?

> I remember sitting in the pew, knowing I would have one hour of calm and rest. I remember closing my eyes and letting the beautiful music wash over me and sink into my being. I remember sharing the reality of mental illness with a few precious church members and I came away refreshed. I held this one sacred hour during the entire week, seeing it as beacon of light that would be there the following Sunday. Then I was ready, although not always willing, to step into the coming week.

> And where is mental illness now in my family? It is definitely still there. I interact daily with mental illness. But there has come acceptance, release of responsibility, and peace. I can look beyond the mental illness, once again to see the beauty of life, in whatever

fashion we experience it in ourselves and in our loved ones. The tsunami is gone, and the waters have calmed.

Whether or not your church participates in a formal program like WISE for Mental Health, the faith community may still provide moments of respite they need. Like Judy, it could be during worship or perhaps it is while in choir rehearsal, or when their child is participating in a youth group or other church activity. A friend of mine who works in children's behavioral health commented:

> If I wanted to have my kids participate in Sunday school or vacation Bible school or whatever spiritual development offering our church had, it was 100 percent expected that I would be there with them—for when they were "disruptive" or needed more support than the volunteer teachers knew what to do. But that meant I never got my one hour of peace and restoration. I've made it a little side mission of mine to make sure others don't miss out on that.

What would it take to create a postcard or bookmark for the pew racks, reminding worshippers that Jesus welcomes all children and likewise to extend grace rather than judgment if a child makes noise or needs to move during church? Beyond that, are there steps your church could take to offer restorative time to stressed-out caregivers?

Praying Through the Tornado of Mental Illness

For some people like Judy, mental illness is like a tsunami. For me, mental illness feels like a tornado. Talking to my therapist, I tried to put into words what I was feeling inside my mind. I told her, "It feels like a tornado. I feel overwhelmed by the chaos. It's like I've put a tornado in a closet because I am afraid of it. I want to let it out of the closet. I want to open a window and let the tornado leave."

I realized the stress of being a mother during uncertain times, along with navigating the physical and mental health challenges for my child, was overwhelming me. Returning to school after summer break is always stressful. This year, in addition to the normal change in routine, we were in a world pandemic and waiting on the results of a possible COVID-19 diagnosis for my child. We anxiously waited several days for the test result - it was negative, thank God! But it was all was happening at once and I felt angry, scared, discouraged, helpless, and hopeless.

My therapist helped me to accept that I could let go of the things I could not control. From years of therapy, I knew this but I needed her to remind me it was possible to let go. Encouraged by her presence with me during my mind-tornado, I began to visualize letting the tornado go out of my mind. Later that night, I wrote this prayer to help me let go of the chaos that was consuming my mind, body, and spirit.

Help me God

There's a tornado in my mind

I've decided to stuff this mind tornado in a closet

It's too messy and out of control

It's sucking all the energy from me

It's getting in the way of all the things that need doing

But maybe you can help me God

Maybe if I close my eyes and cover them with both of my hands, maybe then you could open a window just a crack

Then once the window is cracked open, maybe you could go ahead and unlock the closet door

Then once the closet door is unlocked, maybe you could open the closet door

I will keep my eyes closed and covered for when the tornado passes by

Maybe I will feel something when the tornado is let loose

Maybe I will feel the grief, the rage, the despair, the confusion, the uncertainty, the bitterness, the fear

Maybe there wouldn't be a tornado anymore

Maybe my mind could be set free from these things

God, help free me from the chaos of my mind

I was able to sleep that night after praying this. The next day, I felt better—not perfect, but better. Did the prayer work? Yes. Was it magic? No. It was sitting in the tornado AND therapy AND prayer. With help and guidance from my therapist, I was able to work my way through the tornado and realize I had the power to let it go. The tornado didn't win that time: I did. I am a tornado slayer, not a tornado chaser.

On the one-year anniversary of Sydney's death by suicide, I wrote this poem, which felt more like a prayer.

Stay

in the too quiet room

stay

in the unmade bed

stay

in the folds of the blankets
stay
in the glow of the screen
stay
in the dead of the night
stay
in whatever you need now
stay
just don't leave us
without you
stay

Sometimes mental illness feels like a tsunami, sometimes like a tornado, sometimes like a valley of shadows. Sometimes mental illness feels like nothing. Sometimes all we can hope for is that our loved one will choose to stay.

Whatever mental illness feels like to you, know that I believe what you are feeling. Whatever it is you are thinking, I believe you. You are not alone.

Faith doesn't make mental illness go away; it helps us believe that hope is possible. Faith doesn't cure us of mental illness; it journeys with us through the valley of the shadows or tsunami or tornado of mental illness. Faith doesn't erase mental illness; it reminds us that we are not alone in it.

Mental Health and God-Talk

For faith communities to be a blessing for children and families experiencing mental health challenges, we have an opportunity and a responsibility to reexamine toxic theology and harmful teachings. It's high time for us to get away from viewing mental illness as a sin, a curse, a moral failing, a demon possession, or a punishment from God.

Some members of faith communities have viewed medical treatments for mental illness with suspicion and distrust, and some religious leaders have advised the faithful to throw away psychiatric medications and instead turn to Bible reading and prayer for a cure.

Depression is not a curse or punishment from God, nor is it God's way of testing your faith. Mental illness is a common physical health condition and part of the human condition.

In the conversation about mental health, there is room for both spirituality and science. My spiritual journey includes visions, or visual messages, that seem to come from outside of myself. On the flight to San Antonio the day after Sydney's death, I closed my eyes and a vision came to me. In my mind I saw Sydney moments before she died and she was overcome by shadows, as if she was caught up in a huge tornado. There was something that overwhelmed her, an energy devoid of life. This vision terrified me. I don't know where this vision came from, but I'm curious what it means.

I don't believe Sydney's death was caused by an evil spirit or an ungodly entity. But I do believe that the pain, despair, hopelessness, and desperate sense of needing to escape is a dynamic and complex matrix of elements needing more scientific and spiritual understanding and research.

Instead of perpetuating shame and guilt, it's time for a theology of mental health—that is, a way of talking about God in relation to mental health— that liberates us from the spiritual trauma of the image of an angry Father God who punishes His children with suffering and leaves them feeling abandoned and forsaken. This spiritual trauma stays with people for life. What might such a theology of mental health look like?

A good place to start is to read the Bible through the lens of mental health. In the stories of scripture, we see the human expression of emotions ranging from joy to despair. The Bible provides stories about God and God's people that affirms God's love for us, even when we are in the shadows of mental illness. A few examples of Bible stories containing people who might be thought of as experiencing mental health challenges include Job (PTSD), Hannah (depression), Ezekiel (bipolar), Martha (anxiety), John (eating disorder), King Herod (narcissism), Paul (obsessive compulsive disorder), and Judas (suicide). We can read these stories as human stories in which God's compassion is experienced in the face of human symptoms of mental illness. Nothing can separate us from the love of God, not even mental illness.

The Bible teaches us about God's passion for filling the hungry with good things and God's desire for people experiencing oppression to have their suffering alleviated. God-talk about mental illness talks about the justice issues of affordable, accessible, and quality mental healthcare for all God's people. Mental health theology is a rich area of conversation to continue to explore together for further thought, reflection, and creative conversations. People with lived experiences of mental illness can help us understand what mental health theology looks like and how it can be life-giving and support our efforts for disability and mental health justice.

Spiritual Blessings for Mental Health

Within the lived experiences of mental health, disability, illness, disease, and disorder, we can embrace a spirituality of blessings. We often talk about mental illness as if our brains were detached from our bodies and our souls, when in fact mental health and illness encompasses all of who we are in mind, body, and spirit. I wonder what a mental health-informed spirituality would look like. Put another way, what can mental health challenges teach us about spirituality?

I imagine you can add to this list, but for starters here are seven ways mental illness can have a negative impact on our spirituality. It can make us:

1. Feel as if we are broken
2. Feel alone and isolated
3. Feel unworthy and worthless
4. Feel abandoned
5. Feel as if promises to us have been broken
6. Feel hopeless
7. Feel unlovable

These feelings are often perpetuated by the physical symptoms of mental illness, yet are spiritual in nature. As spiritual beings, we are connected to a higher power, but mental illness can interfere with our sense of connection. Our mental health can benefit from a holistic approach that integrates spiritual teachings with other forms of care, such as medications and behavioral therapies.

Because our mind, body, and spirit are closely integrated, the best outcomes for wellness include an integrated approach. There are seven spiritual truths or solutions found in biblical teachings that can help counter the seven spiritual challenges above:

1. We are whole and created in God's image (Genesis 1:27)
2. We belong to God's family (1 John 3:1–2)
3. We have value and worth as children of God (Jeremiah 31:3)
4. We are always in God's presence (Psalm 139:7)
5. We have God's eternal promise that God will not forsake us (Deuteronomy 31:6–8)
6. We can connect to hope through prayer (Romans 15:13)
7. We are loved, no matter what, by God's Big Blessed Love (1 Corinthians 13:4–7)

Such a spirituality informed by mental health meets us exactly where we are, removing barriers that often get in the way of healing and recovery. Imagine if we embraced a more holistic way of thinking about mental health. Imagine if faith communities taught children these spiritual blessings. Through a spirituality of mental health, we can unlock power and resilience to bring deeper healing to the whole person. Faith communities can be communities of deep healing.

Blessing Our Youth at Church

To be a blessing to children and teens, we can teach them about a God who loves their growing and changing bodies, minds, and spirits, about a God who cares about their doubts, questions, insecurities, struggles, and fears. A God who is free from punishment, judgment, and shame. We can show youth a God who is huggable and lovable. We can give youth a God who is not scary and mean. To paraphrase Lutheran pastor and public theologian Nadia Bolz-Weber, let's stop teaching kids that God killed Jesus because we were bad.[60] Instead, let's teach children of God's unconditional love, no matter what.

The power of faith communities in providing mental health education, support, and resources for families and youth is a mostly untapped opportunity. Since faith communities are often embedded in neighborhoods and can be an integral part of people's everyday lives, they have the potential to serve as critical gateways to health and wholeness. Providing mental health supports in our faith communities removes barriers to mental health treatment.

Coral Gables United Church of Christ in the Miami area partnered with the University of Miami to host a free mental health support group led by a psychologist on their church campus. The service is advertised on their website as a support group for people diagnosed with a mental illness such as bipolar disorder, schizophrenia, and psychotic spectrum disorder. The church describes the service as religiously based and culturally informed. This non-medical environment can be less intimidating and more inviting to people who are sensitive to the stigma and shame of mental illness.

What if every faith community in the United States partnered with a local mental health provider and brought mental health education, resources, and services into every neighborhood in America? What if your faith community had such a partnership? Imagine the youth and families that would be blessed! Faith communities can create spaces where children and teens are seen and heard, their stories about mental health interwoven into the sacred stories of life and our faith.

Imagine youth trusting faith communities with their fears, doubts, vulnerabilities, dreams, insecurities, nightmares, and explorations of who

---

[60]Nadia Bolz-Weber, *Accidental Saints: Finding God in All the Wrong People* (New York: Convergent Books, 2016).

they are as children of God. Imagine a community of faith where youth talk openly about mental illness with each other and with adults without shame or fear of judgment and this openness was valued as part of the sacred stories we share.

While writing these pages at a guest house last summer, I paused to enjoy my lunch outside on a bench in what my hosts call "the pollinator garden." There I saw side by side a hummingbird and monarch butterfly, hovering to take their nectar from the flowers in the garden.

Blessed faith communities are like pollinator gardens embedded throughout our communities. They are places to which we can come to nourish our weary spirits and renew them for our journey ahead. They are places where we connect to others seeking enlightenment and inspiration.

The purpose of a pollinator garden is to reduce the decline of pollinators—in other words, to support the flourishing of bees and butterflies. I love the idea of faith communities reducing the decline of mental health of children, teens, and families, and of them supporting the flourishing of mental health for our blessed youth.

Blessed are the stories, traditions, and communities of faith, for in them we discover hope.

7

Blessed Way Forward

How are the children? Our youth are in crisis.

Mental health challenges are affecting children and teens in ways we are just now starting to understand. In October 2021, the American Academy of Pediatrics (AAP), the American Academy of Child and Adolescent Psychiatry (AACAP), and the Children's Hospital Association (CHA) joined together to declare a national state of emergency in children's mental health.[61]

The pandemic caused the numbers of youth experiencing depression, anxiety, substance use disorders, and suicidal ideation to skyrocket. How are the children? The astronomical rise in suicide rates should be ringing the alarm bells in every school across America.

Environmental factors and negative life events influence our youth's mental health. In addition to the COVID-19 pandemic, the ongoing climate crisis is creating a cascade of environmental hazards that threaten our very existence: fires, flooding, hurricanes, droughts, rising temperatures, and lower air quality, creating weekly national emergencies and disasters. The well-being of the natural world has a direct effect on our own daily lives and stress levels.

Added stressors on our children's mental health include racism, poverty, homelessness, and hunger. Our youth's mental health challenges are influenced by all these negative life events and environmental factors. What if we could better protect our children from the harmful effects of the stressors within our control? What if our policies addressed racism, poverty, homelessness, hunger, and addiction as public mental health emergencies?

Compounding all these problems is the lack of quality, affordable, and accessible mental health care resources, a lack of support for youth, and a lack of hospital beds, residential placements, and trained mental health professionals, especially professionals of color. There is also insufficient

[61]"AAP-AACAP-CHA Declaration of a National Emergency in Child and Adolescent Mental Health," American Academy of Pediatrics, updated on October 19, 2021.

funding for research and treatments about the causes and effects of mental illness on children from newborn to young adulthood.[62]

According to the report by Mental Health America, children and teens know what is contributing to their mental health concerns. Here is what they are saying in their own words.[63]

> I feel so disconnected and confused and alone
>
> Feeling so lost and alone
>
> Feeling like no one else is feeling what I'm feeling or feeling like no one is there for me
>
> Wondering what is wrong with me because no one else seems to feel this way
>
> Not knowing how to get help
>
> I know people who I fear risk suicide, but I don't know how to help
>
> I don't know what's happening to me, but I need help. I'm not ok
>
> Never had enough help to know

Here's what parents are saying about how they're dealing with mental illness in their children:[64]

> I feel totally powerless to help
>
> I need to trust in the professionals to help my child
>
> We want to fix our babies, but we need to accept sometimes we can't and need others to step in
>
> We wish we could wave a magic wand to make it all go away
>
> My beautiful girl now views death as comfort, and I'm utterly crushed as a mom
>
> Guilt will eat you alive, I know...
>
> I didn't have a clue what was going on and carry a lot of guilt for not knowing
>
> It is never simple or easy, but people can get back from a really bad spot

What can we tell such desperate youth and parents? How can we help people find a way forward? Perhaps we can begin by being more transparent

---

[62]Jessica Dym Bartlett and Brandon Stratford, "A National Agenda for Children's Mental Health," Child Trends, January 28, 2021, https://www.childtrends.org/publications/a-national-agenda-for-childrens-mental-health.

[63]"Mental Health America Report."

[64]Ibid.

about our own illnesses and sharing our stories. At least this makes mental illness less of a taboo. And that's a good start.

The Way Forward for One Family Raising a Child with Serious Mental Illness

I believe strongly that by telling our stories, we move forward in our healing. I believe in the power of breaking the silence to help end the shame, stigma, and discrimination of mental illness. Almost every family has a story about mental illness. Some families have several. We need to hear them all. Below is another story from my family.

My sister-in-law Tami shares with us about her journey as a parent of a daughter who first experienced suicidal thinking at the age of 12. Now, fourteen years later, they continue finding their way forward living with serious mental illness, one day at a time. I asked Tami to share with us her wisdom for other families on this journey, and she talked about finding the faith to face each new day. Here is Tami's story.

> Fourteen years ago, my faith was latent, stagnant, in essence a childhood memory of Sunday school and church clothes. I was spiritually bankrupt, an empty shell. I had nothing feeding my soul, and therefore had nothing to give back. I had walked away from God and my daughter's father, feeling abandoned by both of them. It was me and my daughter against the world and I was going to protect her from all the pain and hardship that was my life.

> I was wrong. God never left me. God was always there, and I was never alone. Today, God fills me full of love and grace and light. And because I am filled with faith and surrounded by "my people," I am able to share my story and give back to others. It took me years and many trials and errors, but I found God again and developed a deep, deep faith. I was also blessed to have a few besties that stood by me and endured my rants, monologues, and my own depression as the years passed.

Believing in a God who is loving, who is a healer and miracle worker, who hears and answers her prayers brings Tami comfort and strength for the journey. Tami also finds hope in believing that God has a plan to bless her life and her daughter's life. So each new day, she makes a conscious decision to trust God's plan and turns control over to God. Tami seeks to follow God's will, and in this surrender, she finds peace.

Tami says she also finds hope by developing a network of support.

A by-product of mental illness for my daughter and me was isolation and loneliness. Deviations from routine, people, and situations often caused her anxiety to skyrocket. We always had good intentions but plans with others were often canceled at the last minute. After a while, her few friends quit asking her to join them; she was just going to say no or cancel.

Her mental health consumed my thoughts; I had no time for interests or hobbies. I had to ensure my daughter was ok, doing my best to cheer her up and always looking for solutions for her illness. My obsession became my mindset and it bled over into my friendships and relationships. My conversations with others centered around her status: How was she feeling? Where was she living? (Hospitalized? Home? Intensive Residential Treatment (IRT)?) What medications had been prescribed, changed, or stopped? I constantly worried and wondered—what could I do, how could I fix it and make it all be ok? I alienated coworkers and acquaintances and in general shut people out with my total preoccupation of my daughter and her mental illness. There were no outside interests, hobbies, or events.

The mental illness spilled over and contributed to physical illnesses: chronic migraines, fibromyalgia, and debilitating body pain. It was a never-ending roller coaster of pain. School was a very real and constant struggle and truancy, due to depression and migraines, was our norm. School was hard and the final weeks of high school prior to graduation were BRUTAL: many, many hours "cramming" to finish the already scaled back and missing assignments and tests, attending school for an entire week after her classmates were done, already celebrating their new-found freedom and endless prayer that she would pass her senior year and somehow graduate high school.

God and personal friendships are essential for a full and sustainable life; but they are vital in raising a child with mental health issues. It takes a village—we are not meant to do life alone. Reach out, share your struggles, find support for you and your child outside of the mental health field. I sought out school authorities and talked about our challenges. I was an advocate for my child and am so grateful I was. I met with and talked to my child's guidance counselor, school nurse, and vice principal often and regularly during her high school years. We had a 504 plan that allowed extra time for homework and the ability for her to leave class, if necessary.

By advocating for her daughter and having the support of an amazing network of people, Tami's daughter was able to graduate. Tami says, "She did it! But only by the grace of God and those dedicated educators that cared enough to join us, partner, and walk beside with us on our journey. On commencement day, she walked with her class and received her diploma—despite having missed over 100 days of school her senior year."

Another lesson Tami learned from raising a child and then a teen with serious mental illness is how important it is to not lose yourself in the process of parenting. Tami encourages those caring for youth with mental health challenges to stay engaged in their own lives, make time for hobbies, and not neglect themselves. Much like an airline attendant might tell you, Tami learned from experience that she had to "put her oxygen mask on first" and only then she could help her child put on their mask. Before being able to help her daughter, she had to first address and overcome her own fears.

> I was afraid—always afraid—that she would try to take her own life again. I felt that I couldn't leave her home alone. My rationale was that if I never left her alone, there would be no opportunity for suicide. I didn't want to leave her with anyone else because I was convinced that others couldn't possibly understand, and what if something happened while I was gone? The few times I tried to be a "normal" adult and socialize, I was so full of anxiety that all I could think about was getting back to my child. But people want to help, if given a chance—grandparents, siblings, aunts, and uncles, neighbors, and friends.

> Find people you trust to help you love your child by loving yourself. Practice the art of self-care. Meet a friend for coffee. Go get a pedicure. Develop a new hobby. Make it a habit to eat healthily, get enough rest, and move your body. Candles, cooking, yoga, and eight hours of sleep are my some of my personal favorite forms of self-care.

Parenting children and teens with mental health challenges takes energy and sometimes the focus on survival means we don't have the necessary strength and stamina to enforce boundaries, structures, rules. or responsibilities. Tami has found that letting go of boundaries only contributed to her child's mental health struggles. Tami shares her wisdom about finding a way forward by creating healthy boundaries.

> As a child raised without boundaries, I became an adult without boundaries and a mom without the experience or knowledge of how to set boundaries with my daughter. I knew how to be

responsible, get good grades, and be accountable for my actions, but I lacked the self-esteem and self-respect needed to protect myself from those people who would use and take advantage of me. I wish someone had taught me firm boundaries so that I could have raised my child with more parental authority and daily structure. My daughter has a mental illness. It is chronic and it may never go away. However, a mental illness is not an excuse for not having daily responsibilities to attend to and boundaries and routine a child needs to follow. As with any severe illness, there may be limitations, but responsibility, boundaries, and routine need to exist and be followed consistently.

If I were to do it over again, I would have enforced age-appropriate chores and held her more responsible for helping with meals, grocery shopping, cleaning, and laundry to teach her self-discipline and life skills. She was physically able to do so much more than I made her do, and I believe as time passed she came to believe she was incapable of doing things herself.

I would not have been so quick to let her stay home from school. My daughter is super smart and a voracious reader! I knew she would be ok academically without being in school five days a week—her mental health was more important, right? But I learned that school provides so much more than education; it is also where social needs are fulfilled, and friends are made.

I did for her what she could and should have done for herself. I waited on her and I spoiled her, taking care of her every want and need. I only wanted to take away her pain and make things better by "helping her," but in doing this, I took away her power and her independence. I didn't take away the internal pain she suffered, and I didn't fix anything. All I did was prevent her from learning how to be self-reliable and self-sustainable.

Illness, pain, and tragedy are all part of life, but they are not life itself. My daughter and I have learned to "Live Despite!" We both need to live—despite her illness. We embrace this philosophy and quote it to each other to this day.

As we care for our children living with mental illness, sometimes it is hard to see beyond the illness. Yet we know that our children are more than their mental illness. Tami is finding hope for the way forward by not defining her child by her diagnosis. Tami shares her story of this discovery.

My child is a whole being with so many facets: physical, mental, emotional, spiritual, intellectual, and then some. But I put the mental facet in the spotlight; it was the focus and I allowed everything else to fall by the wayside. As a young child, she loved to swim, ride a bike, play outside, attend dance class, and do karate. For a child or adolescent with mental health issues, especially depression, physical exercise is hard. There is no energy, no will, no endurance, and often medication causes weight gain. I also underestimated the power of color. At her request, I painted her bedroom a deep charcoal gray. It was the color she chose, and it was pretty. However, looking back, I should have said "No, choose another, brighter or softer color." For this was where she spent endless days and weeks and months—in this very dark space with only her thoughts and demons. Don't do it!

I rely on medication to manage my depression, but God gives me natural anti-depressants in the form of sunshine and the great outdoors that are critical to my mental health. Physical activity is also important – whatever form it takes. Enable your child by setting a good example and making exercise and sunshine a daily part of your lives together. Do not forget that happiness, joy, fear, surprise, and anger are still present, along with the deep sadness and despair of depression and mental illness. I thought that if I felt any emotion other than sadness or despair, I would be betraying my daughter. I've learned it is ok to have a good day, even when you fear your child will never have a good day again. It took me many years to separate myself from my daughter's mental illness enough to understand that my child's pain was not my pain or my illness and not to let the weight and pressure of depression drown us both.

A positive attitude, laughter, and sense of belonging brings hope and provides a picture of what life might be like outside of our own heads. It is more than ok to celebrate the smiles, laughter, and brief glimpses of normalcy when they come. When we learn, we grow! I've learned through experiencing different activities, cultures, places, and people. When I don't challenge and stretch myself, I become stagnant in life. Doing the same thing day in and day out without growth is a rabbit hole best avoided, especially when parenting a child with mental illness. Our world is a wondrous place, one to be explored and shared with loved ones.

I've learned volunteering and giving away a piece of myself gets me out of my own head and focuses on someone less fortunate than me. It reminds me that others also suffer, and that life is

not all about me. I believe volunteering and serving is important
to experience and learn as a child, especially when mentally ill.
Volunteering brings about a different perspective. It helps to
broaden a child's view of the world. It exposes them to people,
places, experiences and together you are doing something to
make the world a better place.

Sunshine, movement, and fresh air are natural mood-lifters. If you or
your child take psychiatric medication, spending time outside will only
add to the benefits. And if feelings of being down haven't crossed into
clinical depression territory, a regular practice of being in nature may
be the "medicine" you need. Either way, being outside your four walls
provides a big boost.

Another important factor in moving forward with hope for children
with mental illness is finding ways of being an advocate for our children.
Tami shares her story about the role of being her daughter's number one
advocate.

> Love them unconditionally, encourage them, and know that
> it *does* get better. Sometimes it gets better with medication,
> therapy, love, and support. Sometimes it is all that and time. As
> they develop into adults, their hormones change and their lives
> change, especially if your life is also changing for the better.
> Sometimes it just gets better, or easier because you have faith,
> friendships, and acceptance that you can't fix the mental illness
> or make it go away.

> Seek help. We had an amazing pediatrician who worked
> with us until my daughter turned eighteen, but pediatricians
> can't/won't prescribe anti-depression, anti-anxiety, or anti-
> psychotic medications. Fourteen years ago, child psychiatrists,
> or psychiatrists willing to take an adolescent patient, were rare.
> When we finally found one, we didn't care for him, but we stayed
> because there were no options. And then he left his practice and
> we had to start all over again with a new search. And then again,
> each time having to retell the history and relive the anguish, but
> we didn't give up.

> Today there are more resources available and groups like DBT
> (dialectical behavior therapy) are more common and acceptable.
> We have tried more medications than I could possibly count, with
> dosage variations of every one of them. If something doesn't work,
> try something different. It is not a science; it is an art form. Don't
> ever give up. I give prayers of thanksgiving *every* day that she is
> alive and in my life. My child is my personal gift from God. She

is precious and I adore her. We were meant to do this journey of life together and I am so grateful for second chances.

In Tami's story we learn how one family navigated a way forward with hope while living with the challenges of serious mental illness. Faith, a network of support, self-care, boundaries, not being defined by illness, and advocacy may all be helpful ways to navigate the journey of parenting children and youth living with mental health challenges. Looking forward we can come together and commit ourselves to working towards solutions to the mental health crisis facing youth today.

Solutions to the Mental Health Crisis Facing Our Blessed Youth

My experience as a family member of children living with mental health challenges, as a pastor, as National Minister for Mental Health and Disabilities Justice in the UCC, and as a board member of Mental Health America and Pathways to Promise has provided insight into various options for helping our youth. From what I have seen, the best options to address the mental health crisis facing our youth are to provide mental health education, resources, and support in schools and faith communities.

- Schools can provide mental health education and onsite free counseling services, and form mental health clubs
- Faith communities can provide spiritual support groups for youth and families, plus education and advocacy, and reasons for hope

There's something each one of us can do to help. In addition to working with community-based institutions such as schools and faith communities, as well as advocating to our elected officials, there are small and simple things each one of us can do right now. Rev. Julie Richardson, a mother, minister, and author of *Available Hope: Parenting, Faith and a Terrifying World*, says in her blog post "Dear Parents: Five Things" that even though "it is a terrifying time to be a parent…there are some things that have not, and do not change when it comes to our kids."[65]

Julie's wisdom comes from lived experiences with mental health challenges. She is familiar with the struggles of mental illness in her family. As a mother of a teen and as the loved one of someone who died by suicide, Julie offers us the gift of her testimony and the gift of hope in believing there are concrete things we can do to help our youth. Here are five of them:

---

[65]Julie Richardson, "Dear Parents: Five Things," *Someone Stole My Coffee* (blog), August 8, 2021, https://someonestolemycoffee.com/2021/08/08/dear-parents-five-things/.

Five Things We Can Do to Help Our Blessed Youth

1. **Help youth develop positive relationships with caring adults outside the home.** This is where faith communities can help build a child's circle of support. Youth who have adults they trust beyond their immediate family do better navigating life. The truth is, even though parents want to be the ones to meet our children's every need, we can't. Youth need to develop trustworthy and meaningful relationships with other adults because, as Julie says, it will give them a "better chance at trusting the world, at knowing some of its goodness, at believing they are worth something, at knowing they matter." Mentoring relationships support positive mental health and reduce risk factors for mental illness. Healing happens in relationship.

One Thing Each of Us Can Do

Children: Ask to spend more time with adults you trust outside your family.

Teens: Consider volunteering in a community organization where you can get to know adults who also care about making the world a better place.

Families: Join community organizations where your family can experience "a second home" or a "second family."

Schools: Encourage adult volunteers to connect with students in the classroom and provide opportunities for mentoring.

Faith Communities: Invite church members to think of themselves as mentors to youth. Being a mentor is not just for youth leaders; it's for all of us. Even casual connections that happen on a Sunday morning can begin to plant the seed of trust in a child.

You: Reach out to a youth today.

2. **Help youth replay the soundtrack "I am loved."** Children and teens especially need to hear the words "I love you" at least once a day. Tell our youth they are loved no matter what and that such love is not based on getting good grades or winning the game or starring in the school play. Julie says that most days children and teens "will have a hard time loving themselves. And that means some days they will be very hard to love. But we must. And we must tell them we do. Always and no matter what. 'I love you, and there is nothing you could ever do to change that' is the most important thing we can say to our kids."

After all, it's what God says to each of us every day. "No matter what." Unconditional love expressed daily to our youth does not make them spoiled. Affirming our youth daily will help override any negative thoughts they have about themselves, providing a boost to their mental well-being. Feeling we are held in someone else's mind and heart is a key protective factor for anyone's mental health.

One Thing Each of Us Can Do

Children: Say these words every morning when you look in the mirror, "I am loved."

Teens: Say these words every morning when you look in the mirror, "I am loved." Tell a friend that you love them.

Families: Make the first words of your day, "I love you."

Schools: Share messages of love throughout the school, not just honor roll names and sports victories. Demonstrate love and acceptance and celebrate publicly when students act or speak with love.

Faith Communities: Share messages of love throughout the congregation, "You are loved, no matter what."

You: Tell yourself, "I am loved" and tell a youth, "I love you no matter what."

3. **Help youth expand their worldview.** A normal stage of human development is for children and teens to think the world revolves around them. In addition, today's culture revolving around social media encourages people to be self-absorbed and to always and only present their best self to the world. As adults, we know the selfies and posts aren't the unfiltered, real, and a complete picture. We can help youth by being role models of reality and teaching them our world is bigger and much more complex than the carefully curated social media representations of ourselves and our closest friends. We need to stretch beyond our bubbles.

Julie says we can help youth learn to "engage with people who look, act, love, speak, vote, believe, and learn differently than they do. In a broken, divided, angry and hurting world, to do any less is to do even greater harm." Youth want us to listen to their ideas, thoughts, questions, and concerns about the world. We can help connect them beyond themselves and create a sense that their life matters, that they have a purpose, that they can make a positive difference in the world. Feeling like a valued member of the human family supports positive self-esteem and builds meaning and connection into their lives.

One Thing Each of Us Can Do

Children: Be yourself. Share your ideas. Be creative.

Teens: Take breaks from social media and tune in to others in the hallway or your neighborhood. Remember you are loved, even when you don't look perfect and even when you say something wrong.

Families: Create "tech free" times during which devices are turned off and stored away, such as during meals. Have some conversation starters ready like "What made you smile today?" or "What made you angry/sad/hopeful?"

Schools: Promote awareness of bullying, especially cyber bullying, and empower youth to report harmful incidences such as using social media to shame or alienate others.

Faith Communities: Support diversity initiatives in the community. Promote dialogue among diverse views; host a moderated panel discussion and community forum on important topics where there are conflicting views.

You: Take a youth to the library, an art exhibit, museum, or zoo. Ask them to share with you what they see—what speaks to them and why.

4. **Help our youth hope for the future.** Our children and teens need to know that "the worst things are never the last things." Julie says that our youth need to know that sometimes life hurts, and terribly. They need to know that relationships fall apart, jobs are lost, loved ones die, sometimes money is tight. They also need to know that often adults don't have the answers and we can't fix it, make it better or even make it easier for them. But we can be present and walk with them through the awful and into whatever good and true thing waits on the other side.

This is a companionship model of being with our children even during the tsunami or the tornado of mental illness. The faith community is the midwife of hope for the world. Without hope, overcoming mental health challenges feels nearly impossible. We need one another and we need communities of hope.

Rabbi Sandy Eisenberg Sasso is a faith leader in Indianapolis and an admired colleague of mine who in her children's book, *Butterflies Under Our Hats*, re-tells a Jewish folktale about a town where people grew frustrated and discouraged because no one in the town had any good luck. Yet, even in their struggles, they discovered hope. The butterfly is a symbol for hope and new life. Faith communities are the places where, even when we are down on our luck, even when we suffer from painful life circumstances and illness, there is hope.[66] Faith communities tell the stories of butterflies, the stories of hope with wings.

Spiritually, children and teens need to know that God loves them and does not punish them with suffering. Julie says, "While God does not cause our pain, God does not waste it either, and so, even in pain, there is blessing to be found, most often when we least expect it."

One Thing Each of Us Can Do

Children: Make a hope box, a small container of things that remind you to keep hope alive, such as a feather, a photo, a rock, or a sticker.

Teens: Make a hope wall, a place in your bedroom where you can post images (photos, posters, magazine pages) that remind you to keep hope alive, such as your favorite band, pictures of your pets, friends, scenery from nature, a splash of your favorite color.

Families: Make a hope corner, a place in your home where you can sit and hang out that will remind you to keep hope, a comfortable, cozy place that is relaxing, soft, peaceful, even if it is just a big fuzzy floor pillow.

Schools: Create a place on campus where students can "hold onto hope," a sensory experience that lets them calm down, recenter, and gain peace, such as a garden, a shaded bench, or an indoor corner with soft pillows and sensory supplies such as fidget spinners.

Faith Communities: Encourage members to be ambassadors of hope by inviting others to join them in community, especially reaching out to families and youth. This should be done with no agenda of membership or expectation of institutional involvement—no strings attached.

You: Find your one spot where you go and feel closer to hope. If you don't have one, make one. It can be a simple as a chair that is your "hope chair," a place where you sit or a favorite place in nature to go to recharge your hope battery.

5. **Help our youth find time to act like children.** It's hard for children and teens to be free to enjoy childhood, especially youth with mental health challenges. We can help our youth by creating opportunities for them to play, laugh, be messy, and screw up and excel. Youth are still learning about beautiful and brutal life…if they can hold on to a bit of imagination and wonder, their capacity for hope will be so much greater. Mental illness has a way of forcing our youth to grow up a lot sooner than we would like. It's up to us to create time and opportunities for youth with

---

[66]Sandy Sasso, *Butterflies Under Our Hats* (Brewster, MA: Paraclete Press, 2014).

mental health challenges to be able to feel like children despite everything. All of us need more play in our lives and we are never too old to play. Play is good for our mental health no matter our age.

One Thing Each of Us Can Do

Children: Play is your most important job. Be the boss of play.

Teens: Go outside and touch the grass. Let your mind wander and laugh.

Families: Make time to play together on a weekly basis. Find a family game to play together or an outdoor activity everyone likes and make the activity a priority.

Schools: Provide students with outdoor recess time and institute regular "mental health brain breaks," a mental buffer in-between subjects, even if it is just a few minutes during which you encourage everyone to rest their heads on their desks and you turn off the lights.

Faith Communities: Consider how your property can be used by families and youth in the community for play. If you have open green space, gardens, a playground, or indoor spaces like a gym, host events there for the community.

You: Reach out to youth and invite them to do something fun, such as go to a movie, get ice cream, or go to the park. Make it a regular playdate.

This book offers you many ideas about things you can do individually and together to support the mental health of youth. But probably the most important thing we can do is to nurture hope in ourselves and in one another. Rabbi Sandy encourages us to not lose hope. This is the greatest spiritual lesson of all: Hold onto hope.

Reasons for Hope

We have many reasons for hope. Now that we are aware of the mental health crisis children and teens are facing, we can make a collective commitment to support them better. States are heeding the call to do better at caring for the mental health of our kids, allocating funding to provide school based mental health education, support, and services. Faith communities are creating mental health ministries, providing spiritual support groups, and partnering with mental health professionals to provide quality and affordable counseling services in local communities.

More people are accepting the truth that the kids are not ok. This is good news. The sooner we acknowledge the problems, the sooner we can begin to act. This gives me hope.

Your stories likewise give me hope. While each one is unique, collectively they contain so much love and so many lessons we can learn from and apply to our own lives.

I spoke about reasons for hope with the Rev. Molly Baskette from First Church Berkeley UCC (I mentioned in Chapter 6 that her church is a WISE church for mental health—Welcoming, Inclusive, Supportive, Engaged). Molly is also a colleague, an author, and a mother of children who live with multiple mental health challenges, including depression, anxiety, attention deficit disorder, and substance use disorder. In her book *Bless This Mess: A Modern Guide to Faith and Parenting in a Chaotic World*[67] she writes about the messiness and blessedness of life together as a family. I asked her, "What do you wish someone had told you when you were starting out on the journey of parenting children with mental illness?" Here's the advice she shared.

Children with mental illness are not broken. Molly wishes someone had told her, "It's not your fault. You didn't break your child (by genetics or conditioning), and in fact, they are not broken at all."

Connect to mental health professionals. Molly adds, "Therapists are not all created equal. Find someone who is a really good fit for your child, even if it takes time, effort, and money. Trust your gut and change therapists or clinicians if you are not getting the support you need, if you distrust their diagnosis, if you don't feel they respect you or your child." Consider connecting with a child psychologist, social worker, counselor, play therapist, and psychiatric child's specialist. Treatments may include talk therapy and medication as well as meditation exercises.

Create a circle of support. Molly wishes someone had told her: "Call in all your people. You might worry about the stigma (or suffer from comparing yourselves to 'normal' families), or want to protect your child's privacy, but you need a big raft of people to hold you (and your whole family) up. Call in your pastor, your church ladies, your family, and besties. Besides that, it's ok to tap out here and there. Go away with your partner overnight sometimes. Take a lot of time outs. Cry, rage, pray any way you can. Turn it over to God ('it' being the ultimate responsibility for this beloved person you are so worried about). You can't be your child's single point of failure, all day, every day, forever."

Consider a diagnosis as your new best friend. Molly says, "Diagnoses can help (especially if it gets you an IEP, 504 plan, medication, other kinds of support).[68] Also, don't get too attached to diagnoses. Kids are still

---

[67]Molly Baskette, *Bless This Mess: A Modern Guide to Faith and Parenting in a Chaotic World* (New York: Convergent Books, 2019).

[68]IEP is an individualized education learning plan for students eligible for special education, https://www.courts.ca.gov/35398.htm.

becoming—so much. Think of diagnosis as an assist that they may not 'need' when they reach adulthood." Knowledge is power. The diagnosis opens the pathway to treatment and recovery.

Cherish the children. Molly says, "Listen to your child, ask them questions, hold them tight (if they want to be held). Believe them. Make sure your child knows that you believe them and believe *in* them, and that *you* know they are still becoming. Your job is neither to be in denial nor to catastrophize but to walk the sweet, narrow way of loving them as they are and supporting them into health, stability, safety, and whatever God is making way for next." Molly adds, "One of my best friends from high school, who has suffered from depression and anxiety most of her life, once said to me, 'I feel like if I had just been held long enough as a child and teen, just held with patience and tenderness, that could have resolved most of my stuff.'"

Sydney: My Reason for Hope

After Sydney's death by suicide, her father said that as part of the grieving journey he wanted to "make some positive changes as a result of this tragedy." He said, "I want to go beyond asking for donations for a cause or spreading awareness about an issue." So he is rededicating himself to take a more active role in all aspects of his life "at home, at work, personal dealings and professional." He says, "If I don't ask for help, I probably won't get it. If I don't offer help, some may go without. This life is not meant to be a spectator sport."

One of Sydney's father's ideas, described in Chapter 5, was to share with school administrators about how they could better communicate with students and families about failing grades. Another is to connect to American Foundation for Suicide Prevention (AFSP)—the largest suicide prevention advocacy group in the US—to try to make a transformative change that saves children's lives. He says, "I want to model the AT&T idea of installing factory settings for mental health safety. When you buy certain models of an iPhone the 'Do Not Disturb While Driving' mode is active right out of the box from the factory. Like seatbelts, this saves lives, especially teenagers who may text and drive. This is smart and is good public safety."

He recommends an application, such as the Bark app[69] or something similar already be installed on the cell phone and activated automatically when a parent purchases a phone for their minor child. Bark, for example, can serve as an alert to parents that their child is at risk for harm:

---

[69]For reviews of apps that alert parents to harmful online content, and other parental monitoring apps, check https://www.commonsensemedia.org/blog/parents-ultimate-guide-to-parental-controls.

If its algorithms detect that the child or the person they're communicating with is using profanity, sexting, being bullied or showing signs of depression. The algorithms are also designed to detect threats of violence in addition to discussions of self-harm, suicidal thoughts, or drug use, among other things. The company has found that 35.1% of tweens and 54.4% of teens were involved in a self-harm/suicidal situation. The company has detected and prevented 97,000 severe self-harm situations by sending automatic Parental Alerts when the app detects potential issues, along with expert recommendations from child psychologists for addressing them.

"I would like to see mobile phone companies pre-install this and have it automatically activated for any parent who buys a cell phone for their minor child," Sydney's father says. Rather than having to proactively search for an app and make a purchase or opt in, by having it pre-installed buyers would instead have to take extra steps to uninstall or opt out once provided with information about its usefulness in self-harm prevention, and hopefully think twice before removing the app.

He says, "Sydney had sent text messages about suicidal thoughts to her friends. She ultimately found the method for her suicide after searching Reddit about the technique." While it's impossible to identify any single cause for suicide, we all had to wonder what factors could have encouraged Sydney to at least pause or delay her plans, even if nothing would ultimately have changed her mind about what she planned to do.

If the school counselor had delivered the news to Sydney about her failing grades personally, that might have given her more support in facing the difficult news—especially if the information came along with a human connection and understanding and advice on how to bring her grades up again.

If Sydney's dad had gotten alerts about suicide-related content she was accessing on her phone and laptop, then maybe he could have interrupted the process or had a conversation with her before she got to the point of feeling there were no other options. Could this have saved her life? We will never know.

My mother, Jennie, Sydney's grandmother, took her anger, sorrow, and grief from Sydney's suicide and put it into action. The two were very close. My mother began handwriting letters to elected officials across the country at the state and national level, informing them about the need for improved mental health services for children and encouraging them to take action.

Here is what my mother handwrote on the blank side of a printout of Sydney's obituary.

Dear _____,

Are you aware of the crisis of kids who are overwhelmed by anxiety, depression, and thoughts of self-harm due to the stress of living in these times of school closed, routines disrupted, and parents anxious over lost incomes and uncertain futures?

There is little help for them due to the stress on our healthcare system from the pandemic. Problems like depression become more prevalent in teen years. One in 13 high school students have attempted suicide and at least half of kids with mental illness don't get treatment.

What can you do to help with the growing crisis?

Thank you for your attention, Jennie Griffith

Some responded to her letter. Representative Tom Leeks of Florida's 25th Congressional District said, "First let me start with my sincere condolences to you, your family, friends and all those that had the privilege to know Sydney. My family has also felt the sting of suicide to young adults, more than once." The state representative said that Governor DeSantis had made addressing mental health issues one of their top priorities going forward.

It's important to keep our policymakers—even the ones for whom we didn't vote—informed about our priorities. One of the most powerful ways we can do that is by sharing stories, as my mother did, about how an issue has touched us personally. If you want to learn more about this type of advocacy, there are excellent primers to be found online, such as "Sharing Your Story for a Political Purpose" by Reid Caplan of the Autistic Self Advocacy Network (ASAN).[70]

Many groups, such as the NAMI and others I've listed in the Resources section of this book, offer tools to help users track and weigh in on mental health-related legislation at the federal, state, and local levels. Cole Swanson, a Youth Ambassador for NAMI, grew up feeling as if he didn't fit in with his peers in grade school, feeling stuck and helpless because he didn't know what was going on inside his mind. Cole was diagnosed with ADHD at age 22. As Cole learned more about his mental illness and the treatment options, he realized that mental health was just as important as physical health. Cole says, "Kids want to be heard and understood. They want validation that struggling with their mental health is not

---

[70]Reid Caplan, *Sharing You Story For Political Purposes*, Family Voices, PDF file, http://familyvoices.org/wp-content/uploads/2018/06/2017.4.13_sharing_for_public_policy_purpose-1.pdf.

something to be ashamed of." Cole emphasizes for us a key request we hear repeatedly from youth: "Listen. Really listen to us. Make it okay to for us tell you what is really going on. Help us know it is ok not to be ok."

Dreams of Blessed Youth

I dreamed about Sydney after she died. She was this giant girl walking across the Earth, so tall that her head was as high as the moon, her legs so long that in one step she could cross the continents. In my dream I saw Sydney step off the Earth because her spirit was too big for this world to contain. Beyond the Earth but still part of us, I believe she is still here with us to help show us the way forward. Sydney's light shines on in the constellation of hope.

Even though multiple systems and communities failed her, Sydney believed we could make things better for youth with mental health challenges. We can use our voices and be advocates for mental health education, resources, and support services in schools. We can take active roles in bringing mental health support into our faith communities. We can help ensure these communities do not harm our youth. We all can write to elected officials and demand that they prioritize mental health resources and services for children and teens.

What I want to know now is this: Why did you read *Blessed Youth*? And more importantly, *for whom* did you read it? Who else needs to read this book?

I want this book to change lives. I want this book to save lives. For this to happen, we need to take everything we are learning and apply it to the children that we know and love, and all the children in our communities.

How are the children entrusted to your care? How are the children in your community?

Take a moment now to think of their names and imagine their faces, the sound of their voices. What makes you laugh when you think of them or remember them? What makes you cry? Who is coming into your mind? Write their names down. This book is for you and it's for them too.

We can be part of the solution. We can be the hope for tomorrow. Our blessed youth give me hope because of their courage and their deep belief that they deserve better.

Blessed are the youth, for they are the way forward.

Epilogue

On November 2, 2021, the one-year anniversary of Sydney's suicide, her father shared this reflection on social media with this photo of Sydney. He's given me permission to share them with you.

What's in a year?

a time to reflect, a time to grow, a time to mourn.

it was one year ago that we got that awful phone call.

the one that shakes you to your core and challenges everything you thought you believed.

the Lithuanian word "sielvartas" means "soul tumbling," which is the seemingly endless emotional tumult that is grief.

today we are left with more questions than answers. perhaps some answers are unknowable. we are grateful for the outpouring of love and support, the well wishes and prayers. we hope nobody ever has to make this journey, during this season of suffering, alone.

we are fortunate and grateful to have heard from long lost friends, old acquaintances, and even very extended family from across the decades.

we have shared in many after-church meals, family gatherings, and informal get togethers.

for those informal invitations, we are grateful more than you will ever know.

if you are curious, by the way, while delicious casseroles dropped off at the door are appreciated, their true worth—their treasure— lies in the time spent together in commiseration and expressing the shared experience of loss.

this is what is needed to close the gap between those who have suffered loss and those who have not.

we all need to personally strive to be the force for change that we believe in.

this year, the end of the first year after Sydney left us, challenges us to be true to ourselves and to be honest in answering her call.

we all need to practice random acts of kindness. we all need to strive to give more than we get.

anyone who knew Sydney knew she was a daredevil, the bravest of the brave. She absolutely loved heights, from climbing anything rooted to the ground to soaring above the clouds in airplanes. she was absolutely fearless.

she was also an accomplished scuba diver and sailor. she was an advanced underwater diver who penetrated the deep abyss and captained the most challenging seas. fearless always.

this year, know that there are always forces that protect you; do not be afraid to turn to them in a time of need. nobody is too far removed; we all need human contact and positive affirmation.

today, in remembrance of Sydney, we traveled to her favorite temple in Cheonan, the Gakwonsa Temple.

tonight we entered in solemn remembrance and sat upon meditation mats. We stilled ourselves and heard the call to prayer. We prayed to our Christian God, we recited the Buddhist Prayer to the Deceased, and even recited the Mourner's Kaddish for good measure. In these times, we pray for all people to know the peace that God bestows upon us.

tonight at our home, we held a traditional Korean Jesa ceremony (https://en.wikipedia.org/wiki/Jesa),

"after midnight or in the evening before an ancestor's death anniversary, the descendants set the shrine, with a paper screen facing north and food laid out on a lacquer table as follows: rice, meat, and white fruits on the west, soup, fish, and red fruits on the east, with fruits on the first row, meat and fish on the second, vegetables on the third, and cooked rice and soup on the last."

if you want to review the funeral ceremony from last year, you may find it here: https://www.youtube.com/watch?v=qVQfejPQiHw

many of you have asked how you can help remember Sydney.

speak her name whenever it comes up, do not be ashamed. Share her stories, both her victories and her defeats. help a stranger, care for a succulent plant, eat sunflower seeds.

if you or anyone you know are thinking about suicide, please call 800-273-8255 or send a text to 741741. The Lifeline provides 24/7, free and confidential support for people in distress.

you are loved and will be missed more than you ever know.

treasure today, now, always, and forevermore

Sydney, age 16, at the Gakwonsa Temple in Cheonan, South Korea

Acknowledgments

Thank you to First Congregational United Church of Christ of Indianapolis, Indiana, where I am blessed to serve as pastor.

Thank you to the national setting of the United Church of Christ, where I am blessed to serve as a minister, for your dedication to disabilities and mental health justice.

Thank you to the UCC Disabilities Ministries and the UCC Mental Health Network.

Thank you to the Pathways to Promise and the Mental Health America family, who advocate alongside me for mental health resources, education, and services.

Thank you to conversation partners Pastor Mark Briley, Doug Beach, Rev. Molly Phinney Baskette, Rev. Alan Johnson, Amy Johnson, Rev. Dr. Rachael Keefe, Robin Kempster, and Rev. Julie Richardson, and to the friends and family who graciously shared their stories with me for this book.

Thank you to the publishing team at Chalice Press for partnering with me on *Blessed Are the Crazy*, *Blessed Union*, and *Blessed Youth*.

Thank you to all my readers who encourage me to keep breaking the silence.

Thank you to Beth and David Booram for your hospitality for writing retreats.

Thank you to early reads of this book Rev. Katie O'Dunne, Christine Greenwald, Scott Griffith, Rev. Hollie Holt-Woehl, Cristy James, Rev. Trayce Potter, Rev. Catherine Stuart, Sandy Wood, Callie Yates, Rev. Lee Yates, and Tami Zimmerman.

Thank you to Susan Herman for your support to develop this manuscript and your editing expertise.

Thank you to my mentors, spiritual companions, and friends who hold me in prayer.

Thank you to the therapists and doctors at CenterPoint Counseling at Second Presbyterian Church and Indian Health Group for being part of my family's circle of care.

Thank you to my extended family for the support throughout the journey with mental illness and for generously sharing your stories with us.

Thank you to Sydney's parents for your love and support to help save lives.

Thank you to my father for teaching me about family, mental illness, recovery, and resilience.

Thank you to my mother for encouraging me to write books.

Thank you to Sydney for blessing us during your too short time on Earth.

Thank you to my husband Jonathan and our son Carter for your enduring love and support.

Thank you to God for the ongoing invitation to break the silence about mental illness.

Resources

Encouragement Inspired by Scripture for Youth Who Feel Anxious, Depressed, or Suicidal

Here, I have paraphrased some verses to show how they can capture the types of pain and distress that youth may feel when their mental health is suffering. As a pastor I often say that God-with-us (Jesus) knows every type of human emotion imaginable.

Even when I walk through the valley of depression, I will not be afraid, for you are with me; your spirit of Love keeps me company and comforts me. (Psalm 23:4)

You turned my sobbing and screaming into laughing and dancing; you love me when I'm feeling sad and you love me when I'm feeling peaceful. (Psalm 30:11)

When I cry for help, God hears me and saves me from being overwhelmed by my anxieties. God is with me even when my depression makes me feel unlovable. (Psalm 34:17–18)

God lifted me out of the slimy pit of depression, out of the mud and sludge of my mind. God gets me out of bed and give me energy for my day. (Psalm 40:2)

Why am I feeling suicidal? Why do I have so many disturbing thoughts within me? Put your hope in God and give thanks to God for saving you from self-harm. (Psalm 42:11)

Those who hope in God will renew their mental wellness. They will soar on wings like eagles; they will run even when they feel like giving up, they will walk in self-love and not self-harm. (Isaiah 40:31)

So do not fear having a mental health challenge, for I am with you; do not be overwhelmed, for I am your God. I will strengthen you and help you get better; I will hold you with love and comfort. (Isaiah 41:10)

"For I know the plans I have for you," says God, "plans to bless you and not to harm you, plans to give you hope and a future." (Jeremiah 29:11)

"Come to me, all you who are feeling anxious and depressed, and I will give you rest for your minds. Take my blessing and follow me, for I am gentle and humble in heart, and you will find rest for your souls. For my way is easy and healing for mental health." (Matthew 11:28–30)

We know that for those who love God, all the mental health challenges you are facing will work together for good because your life has an important purpose. Your life matters. (Romans 8:28)

For I am confident that neither suicide or life, or friends or bullies, or things today or things tomorrow, or stress, or happiness or depression, or anything else in the world, will be able to separate us from the love of God in Christ Jesus our Savior. (Romans 8:38–39)

Blessed be the God of our Savior Jesus Christ, the One filled with mercies and comfort, who comforts us in all our mental health challenges, so that we may comfort others struggling with their mental health, with the same comfort we get from God. (2 Corinthians 1:3–4)

Do not be anxious about anything, but in every situation, by prayer and asking for help, with gratitude, tell God what you need. And the peace of God, which is bigger than what we can understand, will protect your hearts and your minds from thoughts of self-harm. (Philippians 4:6–7)

I can recover from mental illness with help from others and with God who strengthens me. (Philippians 4:13)

Give all your anxieties to God because God cares about you. You are not alone. (1 Peter 5:7)

God will wipe every tear from their eyes. There will be no more suicide or sadness or loneliness or crying or pain, for the problems of the past will fade away. (Revelation 21:4)

Mental Health Resources

— American Foundation for Suicide Prevention: www.afsp.org

— *Available Hope: Parenting, Faith, and a Terrifying World* by Julie E. Richardson (St. Louis, MO: Chalice Press, 2016).

— Bark app: www.bark.us

— Behavior as communication: https://www.pacer.org/parent/php/php-c154.pdf, https://www.michiganallianceforfamilies.org/behavior-is-communication/

— Behavior as communication (school-age): https://www.understood.org/articles/en/understanding-behavior-as-communication-a-teachers-guide

— Blessed Mind: www.blessedmind.org

— Centers for Disease Control "Learn the Signs. Act Early": https://www.cdc.gov/ncbddd/actearly/index.html

— Center on the Developing Child at Harvard: https://developingchild.harvard.edu

— Child Mind Institute and Child Trauma Academy: https://childmind. org/

— Childhood Trauma-Changing Minds 5 Healing Gestures: https:// changingmindsnow.org/

— *Depression Workbook for Teens* by Katie Hurley (San Antonio, TX: Althea Press, 2019).

— *Far from the Tree: Parents, Children and the Search for Identity* by Andrew Solomon (New York, NY: Scribner, 2013).

— Interfaith Network on Mental Illness: http://inmi.us

— "It's O.K. to Not Be O.K: 'Gaining Perspective.'" *TIME*, by Naomi Osaka, July 19/26, 2021

— Lives in the Balance: https://livesinthebalance.org

— Make it ok: https://makeitok.org/

— Mayo Clinic: www.mayoclinic.org/diseases

— Mental Health America: https://mhanational.org/

— Mental Health First Aid: https://www.mentalhealthfirstaid.org/

— Mental Health Ministries: http://www.mentalhealthministries.net/

— *How to Talk So Kids Will Listen...And Listen So Kids Will Talk* by Adele Faber and Elaine Mazlish (New York: Simon & Schuster, 2002).

— *My Grandmother's Hands: Racialized Trauma and the Pathway to Mending Our Hearts and Our Bodies* by Resmaa Menakem (Las Vegas, NV: Central Recovery Press, 2017).

— National Alliance on Mental Illness: www.nami.org

— National Child Traumatic Stress Network: https://www.nctsn.org

— National Institute on Drug Abuse: www.drugabuse.gov

— National Institute of Mental Health: www.nimh.nih.org

— National Child Traumatic Stress Network: www.nctsn.org/

— *Night Falls Fast: Understanding Suicide* by Kay Redfield Jamison (New York: Alfred A. Knopf, 1999).

— Ok 2 Talk: ok2talk.org

— Pathways to Promise: https://www.pathways2promise.org/

— *Parenting the New Teen in the Age of Anxiety* by John Duffy (Coral Gables, FL: Mango Media, 2019).

— *Post Traumatic Slave Syndrome: America's Legacy of Enduring Injury and Healing* by Joy DeGruy (Portland, OR: DeGruy Publishing, 2005).

— Steve Fund (dedicated to mental health of students of color): https://stevefund.org/

— Substance Abuse and Mental Health Services Administration: www.samhsa.gov/children

— *The Body Keeps the Score: Brain, Mind, and Body in the Healing of Trauma* by Bessel van der Kolk (New York: Penguin Publishing Group, 2015).

— *The Lifesaving Church: Faith Communities and Suicide Prevention* by Rachael A. Keefe (St. Louis, MO: Chalice Press, 2018).

— The Trevor Project: https://www.thetrevorproject.org/

— *The Whole-Brain Child: 12 Revolutionary Strategies to Nurture Your Child's Developing Mind* by Tina Payne Bryson and Daniel J. Siegel (New York, NY: Bantam, 2012).

— *They Don't Come with Instructions: Cries, Wisdom, and Hope for Parenting Children with Developmental Challenges* by Hollie Holt-Woehl (Minneapolis, MN: Fortress Press, 2018).

— Treatment Advocacy Center: www.treatmentadvocacycenter.org

— United Church of Christ Mental Health Network: https://www.mhn-ucc.org/

— Wellness Recovery Action Plan: www.wellnessrecoveryactionplan.com

— *What Happened to You?: Conversations on Trauma, Resilience, and Healing* by Bruce D. Perry and Oprah Winfrey (New York: Flatiron Books, 2021).

— Yale Center for Emotional Intelligence: https://www.ycei.org

— Yale Child Study Center: https://medicine.yale.edu/childstudy/

— *Youth for Youth Mental Health Guide* Book by Letters to Strangers (Morrisville, NC: Lulu Press, 2019).

— Zero to Three: https://www.zerotothree.org/

National Crisis Lines

— National Crisis Text Line, text HOME to 741741

— National Crisis phone line, 988

— Substance Abuse and Addiction hotline, 1-800-662-HELP (4357)

— Suicide Prevention Lifeline, 1-800-273-TALK (8255), Text HELLO to 7417, www.suicidepreventionlifeline.org/chat

— Teen Text Line, text TEEN to 839863, daily from 6 p.m. to 9 p.m. PST

— Trevor Help Life (for LGBTQ+ youth), 1-866-488-7386

— Veterans' Helpline, 1-800-273-TALK

— Youthline, 1-877-YOUTHLINE (1-877-968-8454)

Trainings for Faith Leaders, Volunteers, Parents, Teachers, and Others Who Work with Youth

— Anxiety in the Classroom: https://anxietyintheclassroom.org

— Companionship Training, three- to four-hour traning by Pathways to Promise: https://www.thecompanionshipmovement.org/

— Mental Health First Aid, eight-hour training: https://www.mental-healthfirstaid.org/takea-course/

— Talk Saves Lives (Foundation for Suicide Prevention) one-hour training: https://afsp.org/talk-saves-lives

— QPR one-hour training (Suicide Assessment): https://qprinstitute.com/

— Risking Connection, two-day workshop: https://www.sidran.org/?s=faith+leaders

For Parents of Adult Children with Mental Health Challenges

Special Needs Alliance (www.specialneedsalliance.org) has a tool to locate attorneys near you for special needs planning. Links to all states can be found on this site.

What Is a Special Needs Trust?

By Julia Kagan, personal finance editor of Investopedia

A special needs trust is a legal arrangement and fiduciary relationship that allows a physically or mentally disabled or chronically ill person to receive income without reducing their eligibility for the public assistance disability benefits provided by Social Security, Supplemental Security Income, Medicare, or Medicaid. In a fiduciary relationship, a person or entity acts on behalf of another person or people to manage assets.

A special needs trust is a popular strategy for those who want to help someone in need without taking the risk that the person will lose their eligibility for programs that require their income or assets to remain below a certain limit.

Judy Smith, member of First Congregational of Berkeley, CA, says:

> My spouse and I have an estate plan that includes a Special Needs Trust for our adult son with a mental illness. This ensures that when he receives funds after our deaths, the money does not go directly to him. If it did, he would lose his public benefits. In addition, we are aware that he would not be able to manage any inheritance, and the money would soon be gone. We selected an attorney with expertise in special needs planning and created a Special Needs Trust for our son.

Notes

Equip the teen in your life to understand and recognize when they are experiencing mental health issues and how to seek help for themselves or a friend. *Blessed Youth Survival Guide* contains tips, important contact information, and a safety pledge to reach out to others if they have thoughts of self-harm or suicide. It fits easily into a pocket, purse or a smart phone's file.

$3.99 / Print: 9780827203235
EPUB: 9780827203242 / EPDF: 9780827203259

For student clubs, youth groups, or community groups, *Blessed Youth Survival Guide* is available in bulk purchases at a discount. Visit ChalicePress.com to order.

chalice press
You Want to Change the World. So Do We.

Order at ChalicePress.com
or wherever you buy books.